The Map to Entrepreneurship

The Map to Entrepreneurship
Your Complete Guide to Being an Entrepreneur

Darwin J. Bruce, J.D.
Entrepreneurship, Inc.

Published by Entrepreneurship, Inc.
P.O. Box 540162, Dallas, Texas 75354

ISBN 0-9786403-0-6
Library of Congress Catalog Number: 2006905349

Printed in the United States of America

ACKNOWLEDGEMENTS

I would like to thank my family and friends
for all their support and encouragement over the years.

TABLE OF CONTENTS

Preface

When I began my legal education at Southern Methodist University School of Law in Dallas, Texas, I was amazed at the amount of information presented covering not only the legal theories and laws that regulate society but also the essential precepts and practical components that compose the operational systems that allow our society to flow and evolve in its metamorphic continuum. This understanding was especially important within the context of business and law. It was at that time that it became apparent to me that a person needs a thorough knowledge of not only the basic parameters of his or her specialty or occupational areas of emphasis but also an understanding of the relationships between business and legal principles that could enhance a person's prospects for success in business.

In my capacity as a business and finance lawyer, I have worked with many business professionals and entrepreneurs to plan, develop, and manage their respective business structures and operations. There are many very gifted and talented people within the American societal landscape with brilliant and creative ideas. However, many do not have the requisite general business and legal background to plan and develop their business ideas beyond the point of starting their business. Those gifts, talents, and skills, with the proper knowledge foundation, can lead to even greater success in the capitalist economic environment within the United States. Entrepreneurial progress should be pursued with passion and knowledge of the basic business and legal principles that compose the system.

Entrepreneurial progress will require a unique view of business and its components, and probably more aptly stated, a unique view on life itself. It is time to understand how to navigate through the economic system instead of allowing the system to navigate us through life. I challenge all others and myself to rise to the occasion and pursue the next level in life and business. Therefore, this book is designed to provide relevant and practical knowledge and information in the synergistic areas of business and law from a unique perspective of inspiration and motivation.

Introduction

◼

The Map to Entrepreneurship

Chapter 1

Introduction: The Preview

It is time to take a journey to a world of opportunity. It is not a geographic location. It is the place where business goals ultimately lead to economic success. In spite of economic difficulties, there are opportunities in the United States for business development and entrepreneurial growth for those who are prepared to seize the moment.

The passion, ambition, gifts, talents, and skills of entrepreneurs can be the underlying ingredients for business success. However, there is tremendous opportunity for even greater levels of success if a person is willing to comprehend and focus energy on developing his or her understanding of the essential business and legal precepts that direct the destiny and entire life of any business enterprise.

There are five factors that are essential for continual growth and development. The factors could effectively apply to both personal and professional development, but I am applying them within the context of business and entrepreneurship to fulfill the purpose of this publication. As in any journey, every business venture must be supported by a purpose, a vision, a map, a plan, and action. It has been my experience that if one of these elements is missing from the equation, any idea or concept will fail to reach its greatest potential.

> **A**s in any journey, every business venture must be supported by a purpose, a vision, a map, a plan, and action.

Every entrepreneur generally understands that a business should be initiated with the purpose of fulfilling certain needs in the marketplace and a vision for fulfilling those needs. Most entrepreneurs also understand that a strategic business plan should be designed to accomplish the objectives of the business. Many do not, however, recognize the importance of developing a practical business knowledge foundation upon which to develop, implement, and manage the purpose, vision, and plan. This book focuses attention on what I believe to be essential information for developing a practical business knowledge foundation for formulating a plan and course of action that will provide the most opportunity for achievement in structuring and operating your business.

When someone decides to become a business owner or entrepreneur, he or she will usually choose an industry in which he or she has special knowledge or interests. More importantly, the person wants to be comfortable in the environment in which he or she plans to provide the service or produce the product. That person's unique service or product in the specific area of interest or knowledge is where all of the passion for success will normally reside. That is also where the passion should reside. However, you will need a map of knowledge through which to navigate your plan to fulfill your business passions.

Every map must be designed so that the reader can understand how to make the most logical and accurate decisions when planning to move toward his or her destination. Likewise, every businessperson must know and understand the landscape of the business and legal environment he or she is required to operate within. A person must also know the required resources for any trip. In business, there is a body of knowledge that could benefit any entrepreneurial endeavor and serve as an essential resource for any business journey.

> This book focuses attention on what I believe to be essential information for developing a practical business knowledge foundation for formulating a plan and course of action that will provide the most opportunity for achievement in structuring and operating your business.

This book is not designed to make you an expert in these areas of knowledge. The purpose is to provide you with insight into the basic concepts and background knowledge that will be essential in planning and managing your business and transactions related to your business. I will have accomplished my goal if, by the end of this book, you are no longer naive, intimidated, or at a disadvantage in any business-related matter as a result of a lack of knowledge of the basic framework of business structure, planning, operation, and growth.

I would also like for the reader to become more comfortable and knowledgeable in these areas when meeting and working with

> **E**very businessperson must know and understand the landscape of the business and legal environment he or she is required to operate within.

his or her professional advisors, other entrepreneurs, investors, and customers. It should also alert you to the importance of having competent professional advisors in handling your business matters, such as a business lawyer, accountant, and financial advisor.

The strategically arranged collaboration of basic foundational areas of information that I believe best serve the entrepreneur is what I refer to as the entrepreneurship knowledge map. In the journey analogy, the entrepreneurship map is the factor that provides you with information about the territories you will encounter and possible experiences along your journey between your departure and your destination.

A map will also provide you with the knowledge and resources that you will need to proceed toward, travel to, and reach your destination points. Every map must be designed so that the reader can understand how to make the most logical and accurate decisions when planning to move toward his or her destination.

Though there are many areas of study and experience that could contribute to business success, I have identified certain areas that are often ignored or not considered in developing a foundation for business. My basis for focusing on these areas evolved from my experience in advising entrepreneurs and business executives. It has become more and more apparent that there is most often failure in certain areas of business development when there has been no plan to support business formation, operations, growth, or increased equity valuation.

In order to grow and develop a business enterprise, the person needs to understand several concepts that could guide and implement its operations. In other words, you would serve yourself well to make every effort to understand the business of doing business. After recognizing and understanding the business of doing business, you can better position your company for growth, development, and rewarding economic success.

In the world of business, you should begin every process with a plan. It becomes very difficult to reach your destination without some plan or methodology for moving in a progressive direction. There have been several books written on the subject of

> **Y**ou would serve yourself well to make every effort to understand the business of doing business.

business planning. There are also many resources available for those interested in gaining more information about the business planning process. Therefore, we will only touch on some of the most pertinent aspects of business planning as it relates to the foundational information that is necessary for your business to build upon.

You are probably aware by now that this a mental journey whereby purpose and vision meet with a plan. The purpose, vision, and plan are propelled by action to reach success. Any person who has a vision for a successful business needs to understand the areas of knowledge and resources that make up the business environment. This knowledge will serve as a map for your journey to business success. This map should then be followed by a solid business plan that is put into action effectively and efficiently.

We are about to take a journey through various channels of information for business and entrepreneurial success. We are proceeding along this journey step by step. But we cannot and should not take a step until we know exactly where the steps are taking us and why. Each step has its own interesting significance. The pages that follow will show us where we are going in business, why we should be eager to get there, the steps we must take to get to that destination, and what to expect along the journey. I don't know about you, but I am excited about the journey and the joy it entails along the way. Let us proceed along this journey one step at a time. Where are we headed? We are headed for success in entrepreneurship.

PURPOSE

1 2 3 4 5

Chapter 2
Purpose: The Journey Begins

The first element in the business success equation is purpose. In the journey analogy, purpose would be comparable to the decisive mindset in which you determine that you want to begin on a journey for certain reasons to reach a specific destination. This element has as much to do with a businessperson's state of mind as it does his or her stated initiatives. Consequently, it is important to evaluate the essential elements of an entrepreneur's state of mind. Therefore, we will begin with a discussion of passion, ambition, and motivation, all of which will affect a person's recognition of his or her purpose.

A practical definition for purpose is the recognition that you have a desire and are destined to accomplish whatever you have been designed to accomplish under a set of given circumstances based upon a definitive determination. I have a passion for advising, consulting, and coaching on the business of doing business.

My passion motivates me to diligently pursue endeavors such as business consulting and authorship on entrepreneurial matters. The product of my passion and motivation is my ambition to be a successful business lawyer, consultant, and author.

I believe that I was created and put on this earth to advise and consult entrepreneurs on the interrelationship between business and legal principles and assist them in their quest for business success. Herein lies the purpose of my business endeavors.

Every person and business entity has to determine the driving force behind every activity. What are you passionate about? What makes you want to focus on a particular effort or subject matter? The answers to these questions are not important for me to understand. The thing that is most important about your answers to these questions is that you have an answer at all. In other words, your purpose should answer your questions as to why you are doing whatever it is you are doing.

Let's briefly discuss passion. In this context, passion is that emotion that signifies your strong desire to pursue and accomplish an objective. When you are passionate about an endeavor, you enthusiastically pursue it in a way that is undeniably driven by your individual desire, not external factors. Therefore, though external factors can be inspiration, external conditions or circumstances should not serve as the basis of your passion. When the passion that exists meets with your ambition, it acts as a catalyst for you to take action to achieve the objectives.

> We often limit ourselves at the very point in our planning when we should have a mindset of unlimited possibilities.

We can identify ambition as the hope that causes your motivation to activate. You may remember instances in your life when you informed others

> ## Limited ambition creates limited success.

of your future plans and they considered you to be very ambitious. Developing an ambitious mindset is critical to your success. We often limit ourselves at the very point in our planning when we should have a mindset of unlimited possibilities. It may be the fear of failure that prevents us from setting high expectations at the beginning of our planning efforts. However, regardless of the reasons, there is no justification for limiting your ambitions. Limited ambition creates limited success.

Without the proper formation of the right level of ambition, the person or entity could lose motivation at an early stage of growth and development. This limited view of ambition and possible deterrence of motivation could result in a faulty identification of the purpose that is the foundation for the endeavors.

Motivation is the momentum to take action to attain the fruits of your ambition. If there is hope, there should be motivation. This is why ambition becomes so important. Ambition is to be perceived at the outer limits so that a continuum of progress can flow with the interminable motivation. Motivation cannot exist where there is no hope or faith in the matters upon

> Ambition is to be perceived at the outer limits so that a continuum of progress can flow with interminable motivation.

which the passion is based or, in other words, where there is little or no ambition.

At this point, you may be wondering what passion, ambition, and motivation have to do with your businesses or your decision to pursue entrepreneurship. The answer is pretty simplistic. As has been discussed, it is my belief that purpose can often be determined by the prevalent passion, ambition, and motivation. We should view business entities in the same manner that we view individuals in terms of being separately identifiable persons or entities. Accordingly, every business must have a purpose for its existence in order to have the propensity for success.

The passion in a business entity is created by its founders. Therefore, you, as the entrepreneur, are responsible for creating the identity and passion for the specific business plans for each business proposed. Consequently, a business can only have as much passion as the founders and managers controlling it. If there is no desire to create the business, you are better off not developing or implementing its plans.

Ambition for a business is similar in nature. Ambition is established by the founders. The founders most often describe the ambition of the business in the goals and mission statement of the organization. As for motivation, while the company is developing, you must ensure that management applies the principles and policies that will direct the company toward its goals. A well-drafted and implemented business plan and strategic direction by management will give the essential motivation for the business to fulfill the purpose intended by its founders.

My hope is that you have identified the purpose for your business endeavors. If you are not at that point, don't worry. Sometimes we stumble onto our destiny by trial and error. But once you determine that you are motivated by a particular thing, or have a passion for a certain effort, or have an ambition to achieve a specific goal, you will hunger to indulge in it. Don't underestimate the passion, motivation, and ambition that may result from discovering this marvelous foundation.

You may be at a point of recognizing a purpose designed solely for you, your life, and your business endeavors. If so, now it is time to ignite the passion, motivation, and ambition in order to attain fulfillment. Everything, including every business, must have a purpose. Once the purpose for each of your proposed businesses is realized, you are ready to formulate the vision to manifest and propel the purpose of each business into existence.

VISION

⓵ ⓶ ⓷ ⓸ ⓹

Chapter 3

The Vision:
A Journey with a Purpose

Once you discover the purpose, you can perceive the vision for fulfilling that purpose through every possible positive avenue that is presented. The question is whether or not you have a vision for the defined operative purpose of your business. In the journey analogy, this would be at the point when you can visually depict the desired destinations for your journey and the routes you would like to take to reach them.

True visionaries see possibilities before they see obstacles because they usually realize that the obstacles are merely opportunities to create new solutions that would place them in a position of continual development and progression. This leads to growth both personally and professionally and is the basic premise people must recognize and acknowledge in order to fulfill the purpose of any vision that lies within them. Individuals have a need to recognize and fulfill their purpose in life. As it is in human life, it is often true of business life cycles in the capitalist society. Business leaders and entrepreneurs who are visionaries must recognize the purpose of their businesses as well as have a vision for how they

> T rue visionaries see possibilities before they see obstacles.

might fulfill the purposes of the businesses. Furthermore, there is no business that can fulfill its purpose if the vision articulated by its founders is without proper development.

The first step in defining your vision is to develop an idea of what you want to accomplish. Your purpose will most likely explain why you are doing something. Your vision is based upon a determination of how far you are willing to go in fulfilling that purpose and the design for how you plan to achieve it. In the real estate industry, a person often refers to phrases such as "design" and "construction" when referencing the major phases of a construction project. A business operation must also go through the design phase. It is in that phase that the vision is created and developed.

I do not want you to confuse this analysis with the process of developing a mission statement or delineated goals for the business. That is a component of the business planning process that will be addressed in a later chapter.

The vision phase should be approached either during or prior to the business planning phase. Remember, the vision sets the stage for the design for the proposed business project. The vision for the business should be as expansive as possible under the existing market conditions. Just as with ambition, a limited vision produces limited results.

A clear business vision should answer questions such as the following: How large do you want the business to grow? What types of products or services do you want the business to sell? How many products and/or services do you want the business to market and sell to the public? What image do you want the business to project to the public? How many locations do you ultimately want to have for the business? Will there be plans for international expansion? What market exists for the business?

Most entrepreneurs also happen to be visionaries. They tend to be very creative and ambitious. Therefore, I do not see lack of vision in itself to be a rarity among entrepreneurial-minded individuals. However, in my experiences, I have found that many entrepreneurs find it difficult to channel their vision.

Creating and expressing the vision are significant factors in any visionary's success. Of course, if those creative ideas are not channeled appropriately, the creativity and expression have no means of reaching the market in an effective manner. Therefore, the following two chapters will give you a glimpse of my philosophy on what I call channeling the vision.

> Creating and expressing the vision are significant factors in any visionary's success.

In order to channel the vision in a direction that is destined for success you should have a plan and a map for the journey. First, prior to the implementation of any vision, there must be a clearly stated and concise plan developed that fully enhances and complements the vision. This plan is one of the most significant documents an entrepreneur could ever draft. Simply stated, it is written evidence of your vision. It is very easy for third parties, including financial institutions, to assume that you have no vision at all if you do not have a written plan for the vision of the business.

Secondly, while supporting your vision with proper planning, you must be aware of the issues and subject matter that each business owner encounters and confronts in his or her quest for entrepreneurial greatness. As has been discussed, I have characterized this phrase "the map" to consist of all of the information and subject matter that is generally encountered by every business. Though various areas of the map will be more applicable and important to certain businesses at different times than others, the map applies to small, midsize, and large businesses whether they are in the start-up, growth, expansion, or liquidation phase. Many of the chapters in this book will focus on the background that you need to effectively grow and manage your businesses as an entrepreneur, which is what I call "the map".

Some individuals do not view the plan and map as channeling the vision of the business. This perception causes a disconnection between the vision and the plan for the business that could result in failure or limited success before the journey begins. Each concept in this book is designed to be connected in some form or fashion to the other elements and concepts discussed. They are inextricably linked. Accordingly, the plan and the map are extremely pertinent to channeling the vision of your business. After all, you want your business to have the greatest chance to survive the journey toward fulfillment of its purpose and to realize the vision for its intended destination.

Of course, it all starts with a vision. Without a vision, a plan and a map are immaterial. You must be a visionary to be an entrepreneur. You must know where the business is going and how it plans to get there. Let's clear the fog. The journey is about to begin. Does your business have a vision? What do you see over the horizon? I see your business with a vision, and its vision is without limits.

PLAN

1 2 3 4 5

Chapter 4

The Plan:
A Blueprint for Success

At this point, you have already discovered your purpose for starting the business and have a vision for its success. In other words, you know where you want to go with your business and why you want to go there. Now it is time for you to plan your journey.

In the journey analogy, this factor would be the predetermined, strategically developed, charted route to reach your points of destination. In the world of business, you should begin every process with a plan. It becomes very difficult to reach your destination without some plan or methodology for moving in a progressive direction. Several books have been written on the subject of business planning. There are also many resources available for those interested in gaining more information about the business planning process.

Even though there is a wealth of information in this area, I would like to discuss the foundation of a well-established business plan and a suggested substantive and structural format for a business plan that can actually evolve at the same rate as your business and the industry in which it operates. Many new entrepreneurs make the mistake of planning for the present state of their business and failing to make the plan adaptive to change in their business structure and operations and/or in the industry.

My goal is to ensure that all readers of this book will avoid this mistake and be well positioned to plan and implement their business in such a manner that it can easily grow and develop while adapting to change. I have assisted clients in developing many business plans. Even though each plan should be tailored to the unique qualities of each specific business venture, there are basic components that should be in every business plan.

I have presented a basic business plan outline below for your reference.

Elements of the Business Plan

The primary structure of a business plan should consist of the following components:

I.   Executive Summary

II. Mission Statement and Goals

III. The Company
     A. Background Information
     B. History

IV. Products and Services
     A. Nature of Products and Services
     B. Pricing of Products and Services

V.   Market
     A. The Industry
     B. Competition

        1. Description of Products/Services of Competitors
        2. Competitors' Strengths
        3. Competitors' Weaknesses

VI. Personnel
    A. Management
    B. Key Employees
    C. Staff Employees
    D. Consultants and Outside Advisors

VII. Operations
    A. Organizational Chart
    B. Divisions of Operation
    C. Departments

VIII. Marketing and Advertising
    A. Target Market
    B. Marketing Strategy
    C. Marketing Tools

IX. Sales and Distribution
    A. Sales and Distribution Strategy
    B. Sales and Distribution Procedures

X. Financial Information
    A. Financial History
    B. Financial Forecast
    C. Financial Requests
        1. Amount of Request
        2. Proposed Use of Funds
        3. Prospective Return on Investment

The business planner should always be able to accurately describe the following through the plan:

(a) the people involved in establishing and developing the business,

(b) the purpose and vision of the business (included in the background and history of the business),

(c) the products and/or services supplied by the business,

(d) the external matters that could affect the business (such as conditions in the market and the quality and quantity of competition), and

(e) the strategies for managing all of the foregoing.

The outline set forth above is just an example of the matters that are covered in a standard business plan. Now, let's discuss some of the nuances to highlight significant areas to focus upon while drafting the plan.

What is an Executive Summary? It is a summary of all of the most significant information contained in the body of the business plan itself. An Executive Summary is an overview of the business plan, and is the first section of the business plan that is reviewed by third parties. It is also the last section of the business plan that should be drafted by the author of the plan. The Executive Summary should follow the same flow of the table of contents in the business plan. The purpose of the Executive Summary is to peak the interest of the third parties by highlighting the most significant aspects of the business.

Critical facts should be briefly summarized to address the following:

(a) the people involved in establishing and developing the business,

(b) the purpose and vision of the business (included in the background and history of the business),

(c) the products and/or services supplied by the business,

(d) the external matters that could affect the business (such as conditions in the market and the quality and quantity of competition), and

(e) the financial position and capitalization needs of the business.

The Executive Summary should clearly state the ideas behind the business and the proposed relationship between the business and the third parties to whom the business plan will be presented.

> The Executive Summary should clearly state the ideas behind the business and the proposed relationship between the business and the third parties to whom the business plan will be presented.

The sections on (1) mission statement and goals, (2) history and background of the company, and (3) products and services offered by the company are fairly self-explanatory.

Be sure to concisely state the mission of the business, which should be consistent with the vision. These sections of the business plan allow you the opportunity to tell the story of the business in its most favorable light. The foregoing sections should advocate for the business in such a manner that you could use the information in future sales presentations.

The section describing the market and its current conditions could be one of the most important areas of your business plan. I also believe that it is the section that is most often overlooked by new entrepreneurs. The most important work on this section takes place prior to writing it. This section requires a tremendous amount of research. You should know the market in which you plan to do business better than any third party who could be reading the business plan. You should analyze not only the potential for revenue in the market but also the quantity, quality, and background of all competitors in the market.

> **Never underestimate the importance of understanding the market in the industry in which your business will operate.**

Never underestimate the importance of understanding the market in the industry in which your business will operate. Such knowledge should frame your strategy for structuring and developing the business both now and in the future. Determine the actual configuration of the market for the business. Identify how the business will be different from the existing competitors in the market. If there is no unique quality in the products and services you are offering, the likelihood of gaining a share of the market becomes greatly diminished. Therefore, in this section you should describe the differentiation between the products and services offered by your company with those of the existing and possible future competitors.

> The personnel section should generally describe the background of the individuals who will be responsible for developing and growing the business.

The personnel section should generally describe the background of the individuals who will be responsible for developing and growing the business. Make sure that the professional biographical profile of the individuals in leadership is sufficient to foster confidence in the third parties that will be the audience for the business plan. Otherwise, they may consider the lack of experienced leadership a mitigating factor in the viability of the business.

A solid flow of operations must also be established and discussed in the business plan. An organizational chart is essential to plan the current and prospective organizational flow of the business. Be sure to include the projected organizational flow that will

> A solid flow of operations must also be established and discussed in the business plan.

be implemented once the business reaches certain levels of growth and development. In other words, anticipate the needs of the business

> **T**he sales and
> distribution
> section should
> discuss the
> logistics of the
> business.

at different stages of development. Not doing so would truly be remiss.

Marketing and advertising are areas that could require the assistance of an outside consultant. However, the business could have participants who have expertise in this area. If not, you should also do a tremendous amount of research on the proper channels for marketing and advertising in the industry in which the business operates. The sales and distribution section should discuss the logistics of the business in managing the prospective sales volume and the process for distributing of the products and services of the business. A brief discussion of this area is often included in the section on operations. But the details of the anticipated processes and procedures should be set forth separately in this section.

The financial section should include existing financial statements as well as financial forecasts for the business. It would be best to consult with an accountant on these matters. The company needs to ensure that all costs and expenses are forecasted. Most entrepreneurs have no problem with forecasting the possibility of large revenue generation. However, the most critical issue for prospective investors may be the amount of return on their investment and the amount of time that could elapse before they could see those returns. In that case, they would be looking at the prospective profit margin as opposed to revenues alone.

As a consequence, the business should not misstate, in any manner, the financial position of the company. The business should also provide a realistic estimate of its capitalization needs. If the purpose of your business plan is to obtain investors or some other form of financing, you must state those needs clearly so that the third parties can make educated decisions on their ability to collaborate with the business in its endeavors.

> **If** the purpose of your business plan is to obtain investors or some other form of financing, you must state those needs clearly.

There are certainly other sections that could be included in a business plan. Do not consider this chapter to be a comprehensive treatise on the subject. But, at a minimum, I think your business could benefit from incorporating the principles from this chapter in the business planning process.

The format of the plan is also important. It must be designed and printed in an extremely professional manner. This plan will often give the business world the first impression of your business. Therefore, make it clear through your business plan that you truly understand the business of doing business and that you are capable of designing a professional and excellent plan.

The cover of the business plan should include a statement that the business plan is confidential and that no part of the plan is to be reproduced or distributed without the written consent of the author. You should always be cognizant of the need to protect all of the ideas and concepts that have been developed in planning your business.

Therefore, I generally recommend that you take the appropriate actions to protect your plan as intellectual property. You should consult with a lawyer who specializes in intellectual property matters before you discuss your plans with any outside party. You may contact the United States Copyright Office and the United States Patent and Trademark Office for more details on certain requirements. I would also suggest that you require each and every person to sign a Nondisclosure and Noncompete Agreement before receiving a copy of your business plan upon its completion.

Prospective entrepreneurs and laypersons refer to the phrase "business plan" very freely. It happens so often that there are those persons who believe that if they put a few ideas down on a piece of paper that they have accomplished the objective of developing a business plan. As you know by now, that is not a sufficient method that would produce results. The business planning process can be long and difficult. However, the efforts incorporated in the planning process will not only be useful for starting your business ventures, but will serve as the foundation for all of your future business development and strategic planning. Consider planning an investment in the future of your business.

You will see that the rewards of diligent planning may easily outweigh the risks of not formally structuring a well-drafted plan for the success of the business. Never start on a journey without a plan to reach wherever you are going. Under such circumstances, you would most assuredly find yourself lost, without direction, headed back to the place where you first began, and attempting to figure out exactly what went wrong. The journey is about to begin. Does your business have a plan? I see a plan for your business, and it looks much better than it looks right now.

> You will see that the rewards of diligent planning may easily outweigh the risks of not formally structuring a well-drafted plan for the success of the business.

MAP

1 2 3 4 5

Chapter 5

The Map:
Knowledge for the Journey

Just visualize any map in your mind. You must acknowledge that every map has identifiable locations, and each location has its own unique characteristics and positioning in comparison to the other areas on the map. In order to take a trip, you must first review the map to determine the best means of getting from one point to another. The map is also useful in making sure that you are familiar with the geographical terrain and climate of each location through which you must travel to get to your destination.

At this point, you should personify your business entity. Consider your business entity as its own person. The business entity is on a journey toward business success. Now let's imagine that the business must have a map to follow en route on the business's journey. One significant difference between an individual person and a personified business is that an individual person does not have other representatives who can travel on his or her behalf in different directions to reach a certain destination. The individual person can only reach his or her destination on his or her own efforts. If the individuals do not do so, then they are not the ones who have actually reached the destination point. However, the map and journey for the personified business is somewhat more expansive.

Unlike an individual person, a business has many avenues of travel that can go in many different directions but be strategically directed to reach one common destination. In other words, a business can have a person responsible for managing marketing, another person responsible for managing finances, another responsible for managing operations, and others responsible for managing other aspects of the business. Or there could be one person responsible for all of these areas. Regardless of the method, they are all different areas on the map through which a business must travel, but they are all headed toward the destination of fulfilling the purpose and realizing the vision of the business in accordance with the plan designed for the business's success.

Through my experiences in business law and business consulting, I have identified certain basic areas of subject matter that I believe must be handled appropriately for a business to have a chance to remain viable throughout its existence. I call these areas "the entrepreneurship map." This imaginary map has areas that represent all of the practical business background information and subject matter necessary to maneuver a business through its various phases of growth and development.

I identify these areas as components of the entrepreneurship map. Along the journey of entrepreneurship, the subject matter components will most likely be encountered by every business at some point in time. In the journey of any business, these components are positioned on the map irrespective of the purpose, vision, and plan for that business. Therefore, regardless of the purpose, vision, and plan for any business endeavor, there are sources of knowledge and information that must be used for strategic decisions to be made. There are also obstacles and barriers that the business may encounter on its course.

The entrepreneurship map covers the following areas:

- **Business Organization**
- **Corporate Finance**
- **Commercial Finance**
- **Commercial Transactions**
- **Commercial and Business Disputes**
- **Corporate Compliance**
- **Corporate Transactions**
- **Business Management**

> **R**egardless of the purpose, vision, and plan for any business endeavor, there are sources of knowledge and information that must be used for strategic decisions to be made.

The first area of knowledge that I believe is critical for any businessperson to understand is business organization and corporate governance. Many new entrepreneurs and business owners overlook the importance of these concepts until a dispute arises between their purported business partners, a lender or financier requires business organizational information and/or documentation, or a lawsuit is filed against the business and the owners realize that there is no business entity properly organized to isolate them from liability concerns. Of course, it generally becomes more complicated and expensive to handle those matters under those circumstances. The best practice is to cover all of the requisite business organizational and governance issues at the beginning of the business planning and development process. It should serve as the foundation for all of your operations.

The business finance area has been divided into two sections. The first section involves discussions associated with commercial financial transactions. This includes any and all transactions in which debt is contemplated for financing business operations and growth. This section describes many types of debt-oriented transactions that a business may consider throughout its existence. This section will also address many alternative forms of debt financing that may be designed for the specific financial needs of a business. We will further discuss the lender and borrower relationship and how a business can best use and benefit from such relationships.

I have subjectively defined the second area of business as corporate finance. This section focuses upon capitalization of a business by issuing ownership interest to investors, which is often referred to as "equity." This capitalization can be accomplished through public offerings, private placements, and other securities-related transactions. It could also involve debt-related transactions whereby debt financing is used to capitalize the business, and some form of ownership interest is transferred to the financier as a part of the transaction.

The financier could receive debentures, options, warrants, or other forms of equity in the business to represent their interests, all of which will be briefly defined and discussed in later chapters.

Another important area to comprehend is what I categorically refer to as commercial transactions. This area encompasses all forms of contractual agreements related to operations within your business as well as those contractual arrangements with other businesses and individuals.

Why is it important to have written agreements to memorialize any contractual arrangement? What are the different types of business relationships that require or justify entering into a contractual relationship? When should contractual relationships be initiated by your business? What are the consequences of entering into business relationships without properly drafted contractual agreements? What happens when contractual agreements are breached or provisions are violated? These are just a few of the questions that will be addressed in this portion of the book.

Most new entrepreneurs do not anticipate encountering legal disputes while en route to fulfilling the purpose and vision of the business. Unfortunately, conflict is a reality that we all must face in life and in business. Therefore, it is best that you are aware of some of the rights and responsibilities of a business as they relate to matters of dispute or potential dispute.

The commercial and business disputes section will provide you with an overview of various claims and causes of action that could be made against your business or that your business may make against others throughout its existence. If you are aware of these issues, you can plan and manage your business accordingly. This section will discuss ways in which to mitigate and/or minimize your risks when dealing with such matters. It will also address how these matters could affect other areas of your business.

Business management and corporate compliance are two separate categories, but they are often intertwined in operational structure and function. It most likely goes without saying that every business must be managed properly to be successful. I will briefly address the areas that must be managed more closely. We will also look at different management structures that could fit the needs of your business operations. Business management is self-identifying. It is exactly what it implies. It refers to the management of all phases of business operation.

Corporate compliance, on the other hand, is the ambiguous phrase that identifies the ability of a business to monitor and ensure compliance with laws and regulations affecting the business in its specific industry. Corporate compliance also includes a business's initiatives to ensure that internal operations are working in accordance within a framework of designated policies and procedures. This area has become increasingly important as a result of the surging number of corporate scandal reports in recent years.

The chapter on corporate transactions is designed to provide an overview of possible changes in business structure that could occur after the business has reached a certain level of development and maturity and that relate to arrangements of the business with other businesses or entrepreneurs. This includes any and all forms of mergers and acquisitions, joint ventures, business associations, and other alternative business arrangements.

This happens to be another area in which business owners tend to depend on insufficient knowledge and understanding. There are major issues to consider when entering into such transactions. Therefore, it is critical that you are familiar with many of those issues that could affect the proper transition of your business as well as the basic concepts that are associated with these types of transactions. However, these are very specialized areas, and you will always want to obtain professional help when proceeding with such transactions.

The aforementioned areas comprise the basic map for the journey of your businesses. Once a business has a purpose, a vision, and a plan, it is time to fully comprehend and follow the map for the journey. With that in mind, let us explore the territory through which our businesses must travel.

> Once a business has a purpose, a vision, and a plan, it is time to fully comprehend and follow the map for the journey.

Chapter 6

Business Organizations

This area serves as the foundation for every business and should be understood by every entrepreneur. Of course, you need to consult with your lawyer and accountant before organizing your business ventures. However, it is important that you understand the advice that they are providing you. This knowledge will also assist you in relating to prospective business partners or associates as well as lenders and outside investors.

Each state in the United States has laws and regulations to govern the organization of various business enterprises available within that state's specific jurisdiction. There are various types of business structures that are available for business formation in each state jurisdiction. The most common forms of business structure are as follows:

> **Common Types of Business Structure**
> - Sole Proprietorship
> - General Partnership
> - Limited Partnership
> - Limited Liability Partnership
> - Limited Liability Company
> - Corporation

We will discuss each one of the above-mentioned structures in greater detail in order to familiarize you with their use and the context in which they could be used. Remember, the purpose is not to make you an expert in business law, but rather to provide you with a sufficient amount of information for you to ask the right questions, make informed business decisions, and have more productive discussions with your professional advisors and prospective business partners and associates.

■ General Overview:

Generally, the best way to understand business entity structures is to identify them as separate fictional persons with their own identities, which are independent from the owners of the business. This does not mean that all of these structures isolate the owners from liability, but it does mean that each business usually promotes and characterizes its existence as a separately existing identity, with the exception of those sole proprietors who operate their businesses solely under their own names.

Limited liability provides protection by enabling certain or all of the owners of the business entity to be isolated from the liabilities incurred by the business organization or other owners of the business. Commonly, the following business structures are the only structures that provide limited liability: corporation, limited liability company, limited partnership (only the limited partners have limited liability), and limited liability partnership (owners have limited liability protection from the liabilities incurred by the other owners of the organization and not those incurred by the business entity itself). Therefore, it is evident that separately identifying a business alone does not connote isolation from liability unless an appropriate entity structure is used to accomplish this task.

Of course, there are many other factors to consider, in addition to limited liability protection, in determining the appropriate business entity structure for your proposed business endeavors. These factors and other considerations are discussed in more detail at the end of this chapter under the section subtitled "Choice of Entity." However, it is best to understand the basic characteristics of each of the possible business structures before analyzing the possible choices for business formation. We will start with the sole proprietorship structure.

Sole Proprietorship

A sole proprietorship is a business structured with one owner who assumes all of the risk and liability associated with the business, but who also captures any and all profits earned by the business. Sole proprietorships are generally operated under an assumed name in lieu of using the individual name of the owner. The owner usually files an assumed name certificate in his or her state and local jurisdiction in order to have the owner's business identified under a separate business name that has been created for the business by the owner. There are generally no specific organizational or formation documents or filing requirements with the state jurisdiction for establishing and operating this form of business.

However, the owner must be sure that he or she has obtained all of the required permits, licenses, or certifications that may be required to perform services or produce materials in the specific industry in which the business intends to provide services or products. All industry-specific regulatory requirements must be met regardless of the entity structure chosen. Regulatory and other forms of compliance will be discussed in greater detail in the chapter on corporate compliance.

A sole proprietorship does provide the greatest degree of independence, freedom, and flexibility for the business owner, but it could also provide the greatest degree of risk. I generally do not recommend this entity structure unless the owner is absolutely sure that he or she is willing to assume all of the risks of the business affairs and be able to account for the unlimited liability potential from business operations. These risks may be minimized with insurance protection, but it is rare that insurance products can alleviate all risks associated with a business venture.

Partnership

A partnership can basically be described as a business conducted similarly to a sole proprietorship with more than one owner. A partnership is sometimes referred to as a general partnership in order to differentiate it from the other types of partnership structures. Two or more individuals or entities that actively participate in the management and day-to-day operations of a business form a partnership. There are also no specific organizational documents or filing requirements with the state jurisdiction to establish this form of business.

However, the owners may execute a partnership agreement to set forth all of the rights of the partners and general guidelines for operating the partnership. Although it is not required for the partners to enter into any such agreement for the partnership to be effective, it is strongly encouraged. I would not recommend that anyone enter into a partnership arrangement without formalizing the relationship with a written partnership agreement.

Each state has laws and regulations that govern the structure and operation of partnerships. These laws are generally applicable only in the absence of a written partnership agreement or when addressing issues not covered in a written agreement between the parties. Accordingly, there are prospective and existing partners who rely on these statutes and rules to protect their interests in the general partnership arrangement.

However, I have counseled many clients on dispute-related matters that are the result of not formalizing a partnership relationship in writing. Many of the issues they faced could have been avoided if they had simply planned the business arrangement in writing from the outset. If they don't, the statutes of the state in which the business is in operation may apply, and the only resolution to a dispute would be to seek a ruling from a court of competent jurisdiction as opposed to understanding the relationship of the parties through a written partnership agreement and most likely resolving the matter among themselves.

A general partnership does not provide limited liability protection for its owners. The owners of a partnership are jointly and severally liable for any and all debts and liabilities incurred by the partnership. This means that each and every partner is responsible for all debts and liabilities of the partnership. Therefore, the issues and concerns of total risk assumption also apply to general partnerships in the same manner that they apply to the sole proprietorship structure.

It is also important to understand that a partnership can consist of a partnership of other business entities. The general partnership structure is not limited to individual persons. Other businesses with different business structures can also be partners in a partnership. Corporations can be partners. Limited liability companies can be partners. The possibilities are varied, which allows for creative and effective business planning.

As with other business entities, a partnership can also be converted into a different entity structure if the partners so desire. This is a common strategy used by partnerships after they have achieved a certain level of growth. Many convert to an entity with limited liability protection or that can provide the basis for selling marketable investment securities related to the business. Of course, the general partnership can be a successful form of business operation on its own merit if organized and managed appropriately.

Limited Liability Partnership

A limited liability partnership is very similar to a general partnership. As with a general partnership, this entity structure does not isolate the owners from liabilities incurred by the entity itself. However, this is a structure that does allow two or more individuals to form and operate a business providing limited liability protection for each owner from any liabilities caused by the other owners in the business. These entity structures are quite common in professional service firms, where there is often concern over isolating each professional's potential malpractice or other liability exposure from the other professionals' participating in the business arrangement.

Limited liability partnerships should also be operated in conformity with a written limited liability partnership agreement. The owners can formulate the terms of the agreement to best suit the needs of the business operation and to set forth the obligations, rights, and responsibilities of each of the owners in the business structure.

Generally, there are filing requirements for businesses that operate as registered limited liability partnerships. They must be registered in the office of the state in which the business operates. There are basic regulatory requirements for limited liability partnerships as well. The requirements are not as extensive as those required for corporations, but you should gain some familiarity with the laws and regulations that govern this type of entity in the jurisdiction in which you operate your business if you intend to establish this entity structure.

Limited Partnership

The formation of this entity often involves a fairly complex combination of individuals and other entity structures. It therefore involves a more centralized method of management compared to the general or limited liability partnership. A limited partnership is often the entity of choice for those who wish to structure a business that is capitalized by passive investors, but have a need for one individual or entity to accept all of the responsibility and risks of exposure in operating the business enterprise. In other words, most of the money and other resources needed to start and operate the business are obtained by individuals or entities that will not be active participants in managing the affairs of the business. This entity is very prevalent in the real estate industry and is often used to attract private real estate investors.

A limited partnership is formed by a general partner, which is an individual or entity that assumes any and all liability for the business. The general partner then admits limited partners into the business with shares or units of interest based upon their contributions to the limited partnership. The limited partners are not active in managing or operating the business but generally receive a percentage of return on their investment in the limited partnership that is often related to the amount, value, or percentage of their initial contribution to the limited partnership.

The limited partners also have limited liability. They are only liable in the limited partnership to the extent of their capital contributions to the limited partnership. Therefore, often the worst-case scenario for a limited partner in a limited partnership is the loss of the money or property contributed to the business. In most states, the general partner must file a certificate of limited partnership or similar document with the state agency to register the limited partnership to operate in that particular state.

It is common for the general partner to be a separate entity such as a corporation or limited liability company in order to provide liability protection for the owners who are responsible for managing and handling the daily affairs of the business as the general partner. It is also common for the general partner to hold a nominal number of shares of interest in the limited partnership while the limited partners hold the majority of equity (ownership) interest in the entity. This practice places all of the liability on the owner with the least amount of equity interest and provides the greatest benefit to those owners with limited liability and the greatest amount of equity interest.

Corporation

At the risk of sounding redundant, I must reiterate that the most important concept about corporations that a businessperson should understand is the fact that a corporation is a separate identifiable entity that is wholly remote and independent from its owners. I often explain the nature of a corporation as a separate

---

identifiable person. Even though it is its own entity to itself, the corporation has structural components that supply the resources and the purpose for its existence. The basic corporate structure consists of the following:

(1) shareholders,

(2) board of directors, and

(3) officers.

Shareholders are the owners of the corporation. Their ownership in the corporation is represented by shares of interest indicating the amount of equity held by each shareholder. The members of the board of directors are responsible for designing the vision and strategy for the corporation. The officers are responsible for overseeing the day-to-day operations of the corporation.

Corporations are formed by an incorporator filing Articles of Incorporation, also known as Articles of Formation, with the Secretary of State or other regulatory agency that governs business formation in the state in which the corporation will have its existence. The articles usually include, at a minimum, the designation of the board of directors, the purpose of the corporation, the name and address of the registered agent for the corporation, and the number of shares that will be authorized for issuance by the board of directors.

The state agency will then issue a certificate acknowledging the existence of the newly formed corporation and that the articles have been approved and found to comply with the laws of the state.

The initially designated board of directors then must have an organizational meeting to approve the requisite actions for the corporation's initial organizational matters. This involves addressing many issues of governance, including the approval of the bylaws of the corporation, which is a document promulgated and acknowledged by the board of directors or secretary to establish the policies and procedures for governing the internal operational structure of the corporation.

The shareholders and board of directors in the corporate structure must also hold meetings as required in the bylaws or by the laws of the state of the corporation's existence. Shareholders generally elect the board of directors, excepting the initial board of directors. The board of directors elects the officers of the corporation. In most states, the required officer positions are president, secretary, and treasurer. Other officers may also be appointed. Matters resolved in a meeting may also be handled by the written unanimous consent of all parties where allowed in the bylaws or state laws.

Corporations provide limited liability protection for the shareholders. This simply means that the owners of interest in a corporation are not personally liable for the debts and other obligations of the corporation.

Of course, one of the greatest advantages of the corporate structure is the ability to issue additional shares of interest to new shareholders in an effort to raise capital for the business. The corporate entity is often the most viable option for meeting this need due to its broad acceptance in the investing business community. A corporation is also the entity considered the most marketable when considering to sell the business's equity on the publicly traded securities markets. There will be more discussion about these topics in the chapter on corporate finance.

The corporation also has two distinct category types of formation. A corporation may be classified as a C-corporation or an S-corporation. The differentiation is significant only with regard to the entity's status under the federal tax laws. Therefore, the identification is made with the Internal Revenue Service. A C-corporation is taxed as a separate entity, and its shareholders are also taxed for gains received from the corporation. An S-corporation is not taxed as a separate entity, and all tax liability passes through directly to the shareholders. All corporations are initially identified as C-corporations unless the appropriate form (Form 2553) is filed with the Internal Revenue Service requesting that the entity be classified as an S-corporation.

As previously discussed, this entity has more requirements for maintaining its existence than the other entity structures. Failure to comply with the legal requirements in the respective state jurisdiction could result in the involuntary dissolution of the corporate business entity. Therefore, it is important for the participants in the corporate venture to understand the basic requirements for forming, operating, and maintaining the corporate structure accordingly.

Limited Liability Company

A limited liability company is now considered one of the most popular forms of business organization by many new entrepreneurs. It provides most of the characteristics of flexibility that are present in the partnership structure, but also provides many of the desirable characteristics of the corporate structure. Many understand a limited liability company better as a hybrid between the two structures. I happen to be a big proponent of this business structure for those entrepreneurs who desire to have limited liability protection for all owners and a pass-through tax structure, but not have the limitation on the number of shareholders, as in an S-corporation.

A limited liability company is structured and governed in a manner that is very similar to that of a corporation. A limited liability company consists of the following:

(1) members, who are comparable to shareholders in a corporation;
(2) managers, who are comparable to the board of directors of a corporation; and
(3) officers, those who manage the organization.

Filing organizational documents with the appropriate state regulatory agency forms the limited liability company. It generally has an internal document that manages its governance that is called the operating agreement or regulations, which is similar to bylaws of a corporation. These documents most often require meetings to be held and minutes to be drafted to reflect the resolutions promulgated by the members or managers at their requisite meetings.

As with corporations, a limited liability company is a separate identifiable entity. It also possesses its own identity apart from its owners.

The nomenclature for the limited liability company can be quite different depending on the jurisdiction in which you form the entity. Of course, there are many state legislatures that have worked to bring uniformity in the terminology used by all business entity forms. The state of Texas is a good example. Texas has recently enacted the new Texas Business Organizations Act. This new act became effective January 2006. The new legislation provides for more clarity on the definitions and identification within various entity structures.

Both limited liability companies and S-corporations can have pass through tax treatment for IRS tax purposes. Regardless of the need to understand different terminology, there are simply two main differences between limited liability companies and S-corporations that you may need to know to make the appropriate organizational decision. First, the shares of an S-corporation can only be owned by individual persons. An S-corporation is not allowed to have another corporation, limited liability company, trust, or any other form of business entity to have ownership of its shares of interest. Secondly, an S-corporation is limited to no more than 75 shareholders. A limited liability company is not subject to the foregoing limitations.

This is why it is has been the entity of choice for many newly formed small business entities that anticipate and desire growth.

Agreements Between Owners

■ Partnership Agreement:

The Partnership Agreement not only serves as the foundation for the relationship between partners in a partnership, it also serves as the foundation for the governance and operation of the partnership business entity itself. Since a partnership does not have bylaws as a corporation, the partnership agreement must include all of the rules and policies that are necessary for efficiently managing the internal structure of the business.

It is not mandatory to have a written partnership agreement. Under such circumstances, the rules and statutes in the state in which the partnership will operate will govern the entity. However, I must caution any individual who desires to form a partnership without a written partnership agreement. I believe entering into a partnership without a partnership agreement could be the most costly business organization mistake an entrepreneur could ever experience. The most common legal dispute matters that I have addressed in my practice have revolved around the failure of entrepreneurs to formalize their business relationship in writing.

This practice not only creates a potential environment for business litigation, but it allows unscrupulous individuals the opportunity to cause damages to the business and the other partners before the civil legal system can address any issues appropriately. Therefore, in many cases the damage has already been maximized before the laws can be used to protect the interests of the partners who have been victimized.

Another downside to taking chances in a partnership without an agreement is the amount of expense associated with civil litigation. Legal services and costs are often very expensive in business litigation. In many cases, it may not be financially prudent to even pursue the matters if the expenses are vast and the assets of the defendants or prospective defendants are limited or have nominal value. Therefore, I always recommend that prospective partners enter into a comprehensive partnership agreement under any circumstances and regardless of any preexisting relationship between the partners.

Aside from the partnership agreement, it may be necessary for the partnership to acquire an assumed name to identify the business. The partners must file an assumed name certificate in the state and county offices in which the partnership operates in order to claim an assumed name for the business.

■ Limited Partnership Agreement:

This agreement also serves as the foundation for its entity's existence. The agreement for the limited partnership has an even greater significance. It must describe the various types of limited partnership interests, the relationship between the general partner and the limited partners, the tax consequences associated with ownership interests in the limited partnership, the relationship between the limited partners, as well as other matters associated with the proper governance of the business.

Since limited partnership interest can easily be characterized as a "security" as defined in the context of investments, there are many other securities regulation issues that must be considered when forming these entities. Consequently, the limited partnership agreement will likely address the basic framework for compliance with the securities and other applicable laws and regulations.

If interests in the limited partnership will be sold to capitalize the entity, it may be necessary to prepare securities offering documents, such as a prospective investor questionnaire, private placement memorandum (sometimes referred to as a "Prospectus"), subscription agreement, and other related materials. The purpose of securities offering documents is to fully inform the prospective investor of the risks of the investment and give a comprehensive background of the company and the business interests. Securities offering documents are applicable to any business entity structure that seeks to capitalize its operations by selling equity interests in the business. This area will be discussed in greater detail in the chapter on corporate finance.

A limited partnership must also file a certificate of limited partnership with the secretary of state in the state in which the business is formed. This document must be prepared in addition to the limited partnership agreement. The certificate of limited partnership is a basic document that generally requires only the name and address of the general partner and the duration of the limited partnership and other administrative information.

■ Shareholder Agreements:

I believe that Shareholder Agreements are essential for small business owners. This may be one of the most unrecognizable issues for small business entrepreneurs. Many new entrepreneurs realize that some form of structure and organization is needed to manage the affairs of the business properly. Hopefully, the information in this book will assist in the process as well.

However, you must not forget that even though the issues are handled concerning the governance of the business entity and its structure and objectives, there are potential outstanding issues concerning the individual relationships between the shareholders that may not have been covered in the Formation documents or Bylaws of the corporation. Therefore, the Shareholder Agreement may be a very critical and essential document to address these matters appropriately.

The Shareholder Agreement is the document that covers the issues related to the restrictions on the transfer of business interests in a corporation. This document should describe the process allowed for transfer of the interests during the existence of the corporation as well as the process for disposition upon dissolution of the corporation, death of a shareholder, or any other event terminating the shareholder's ownership relationship with the corporation.

The Shareholder Agreement may also be useful in protecting the rights of minority shareholders (those shareholders who own less than fifty percent of the outstanding shares of stock in the corporation). Even though such matters can be covered in the Bylaws or Formation documents, the Shareholder Agreement may be preferable in order to establish a formal framework that deals only with issues associated with the relationships between the shareholders and no other matters.

Choice of Entity

There are several factors to be considered when determining the most appropriate business structure for your business ventures. The factors most often considered are as follows:

- The number of owners in the business

- Whether owners will be active participants in the business or passive investors

- How the entity and the owners will be taxed

- The ability of the entity to protect owners of the business from liabilities arising out of business operations

- The formalities associated with the business structure

- The desired management structure of the business

- The ability and flexibility of raising capital to fund initial business operations

- The efficient transferability of ownership interests in the business

- The vision and goals of the business owners for business growth and development

- The exit strategy contemplated by the founding business owners

- The continuity of life of the business entity formed

There are certain basic questions that I ask every person who is either starting a business or creating a proper foundation for existing business operations: What is your vision for the business in the areas of initial operation, growth, development, exit strategies, and personal involvement of the founders? It may sound strange, but these issues are very important to address while structuring your business at the outset. It is very difficult to design a business plan if you do not know exactly where you are trying to go with the business itself. A wise entrepreneur should know the ultimate desired destination for the business and its founders.

In addition to the factors specified above, a business may need to consider a multi-entity structure to isolate liabilities and differentiate between divisions of products or services or geographic locations of a business. A multi-entity structure is simply the use of more than one form of business structure contemporaneously in a multi-level format with each entity structure contributing to the cooperative fulfillment of the purpose and vision for the business venture.

Multi-entity structures are most commonly used with the corporate business structure, but could also be used with partnerships and limited liability companies if it is legally permissible when statutory and regulatory limitations are considered. The possible combinations are varied and could be creatively designed in whatever manner desired by the leadership within the requisite legal parameters. Of course, you should be sure that the structural design ultimately acts in the best interest of the vision for the business venture.

A corporation owning other corporations or any other form of entity is an example to consider. The corporation that holds the ownership would be identified as the parent corporation, and the entity owned would be identified as the subsidiary entity. Another example is a limited liability company owning limited partnership interests in a limited partnership.

There are many different reasons for structuring business ventures in multi-entity structures. As a company grows and expands its operations, it may be beneficial to place a separate division of operation for the business into its own entity structure so that the assets and liabilities of the separate division could be more easily isolated. An additional rationale for using a separate structure could be the need to structure a joint venture of limited duration with another company that needs to remain remote in its operation. This would allow the business conglomerate to benefit from external operations yet isolate the responsibilities and liabilities of the separate entity.

The process of evaluation should be the same regardless of the choice of business entity or the various combinations of entities. The entrepreneur should first be sure that the vision and purpose for the business are thoroughly understood and established, the aforementioned choice of entity factors are considered, and a comprehensive business plan is prepared to document the purpose and the vision accordingly.

Chapter 7

Corporate Finance

This section characterizes corporate finance as any and all mechanisms used to capitalize the business enterprise. In other words, the business must have enough financial and other economic resources available to begin and support the start-up operations. Initial capitalization may consist of money, property, or service contributions of investors. The configuration of these contributions generally determines the equity structure of the business. The founders of the business often determine the contributions each will make to the business and structure ownership based upon those determinations.

Many business financing issues evolve out of the organizational structure of the business. Therefore, we would be remiss to address the equity structure of the business without evaluating the capitalization needs that are required to support the business based upon the chosen entity structure.

Sole Proprietorship

The sole proprietorship is, by its very nature, capitalized by the owner of the business either by use of the owner's assets or the owner incurring personal debt to capitalize the business. The sole proprietorship is unable to obtain outside investors who have ownership in the business because the basic premise of this type of entity is that it consists of one sole owner. The owner often either saves the amount of money to start the business enterprise or borrows funds from family and/or friends until the business is able to make a profit and the debts can be repaid.

Partnership and Limited Liability Partnership

As discussed in the previous chapter, the partnership and the limited liability partnership are very similar structures. The main structural difference is in the fact that the partners in a limited liability partnership are isolated from the individual liabilities of the other partners. Otherwise, these entities generally function in the same manner.

The partnership agreement should set forth the allocation of each partner's percentage of sharing in the profits and losses of the business. This percentage is often determined by comparing the capital contributions of each partner to the business. The partner's capital contributions could consist of money, property, or services. Of course, the total capitalization, regardless of the assets contributed by each partner, has to be sufficient in the aggregate to support the operations of the business. If not, other or additional partners may be considered or the required capitalization can be reduced or modified in some manner.

Both the partnership and the limited liability partnership can be capitalized by the assets of the partners in the organization. These partners may also borrow funds from others to obtain their capital contribution. However, just as with the sole proprietorship, the partner will most likely be required to repay the amounts borrowed since no person or entity outside of the partnership can receive ownership interests without being a partner itself. Otherwise, other partners may be added to provide the necessary capital infusion into the business, but this approach could possibly require the existing partners to dilute their ownership interests in the partnership.

Limited Partnership

The limited partnership is a somewhat unique entity. A limited partnership must have a general partner to function as an entity. The general partner assumes all liability for the limited partnership enterprise and is responsible for all business operations, but is not generally responsible for capitalizing the business. Most of these organizations are capitalized by contributions from the limited partners. The limited partners in the limited partnership are called passive investors. Limited partners must remain passive and not be involved with the operations of the business in order to maintain their limited liability protection and thus avoid being subject to the liabilities of the business entity.

This is an important concept for several reasons. Limited partner investments are the essential driving force for organizers to form a limited partnership. In addition, the desired benefit to the limited partners is to have an opportunity to obtain a return on their investment while only risking the amount of their investment and incurring no other liabilities of the business. The structure is designed to fit the economic relationship between the parties in financing and operating the business.

The amount of ownership interests allocated among the parties will vary depending on the amount of capital necessary to support the business, the number of limited partners involved, the amount of capital and resources contributed by the general partner, the proposed return on investment for the limited partners, and other ancillary factors. These allocations should be specifically described in the limited partnership agreement.

Corporation

In order to capitalize the business, founders of a corporation may depend upon the sale of equity or the sale of debt. The first method is the sale of ownership interests in the corporation to various individuals or entities. This ownership interest in the corporate entity is called equity. The equity interest is identified as shares of stock in the corporation.

The amount of equity received by investors is determined by the amount of shares of stock acquired in exchange for some form of value contributed to the capital of the corporation. This value could consist of money, services, and/or property contributed to the corporation. However, the Board of Directors usually retains the right to accept or decline any form of contribution.

Most often, capitalization of the corporate structure is associated or deemed to be synonymous with the phrase corporate or business finance. This could be the result of exposure of the securities market to the general public through business and national news media. Individuals also rely heavily upon corporate financial products in developing their personal investment portfolio or strategy.

Whatever the reasoning, most individuals and investors are only familiar with one type of business financial product called common stock or shares of common stock. We will briefly discuss other forms of equity that a corporation could issue to its investors. We will also discuss many of the factors that should be considered when determining the types of equity that should be offered by a business to satisfy its capitalization needs as well as fulfill the market needs of the investors.

There are different forms of equity that can be sold by a corporation to assist in financing its business endeavors. The basic forms of equity are common stock, preferred stock, and convertible preferred stock. Common stock gives the owner the right to fully participate in the profits of the corporation and any increases in value in the corporation's equity. Common stock generally comes with voting rights associated with the ownership interests. Most individuals are familiar with this type of equity because it is the form most likely to be in their investment portfolios.

Another type of equity is called preferred stock. Preferred stock is equity that has preference in payment of dividends. If there are profits generated by the company and the leadership of company chooses to disburse dividend payments, the holders of preferred stock are paid dividends prior to any payments to the common shareholders.

However, preferred stockholders do not generally have voting rights. An additional consideration is that the dividend payments are made only when a company generates profits. Preferred stockholders could find themselves in a position where there is no profit for dividend distribution, and they have no voting rights to affect change in the management of the company. For this reason, it is often difficult to find preferred stock investors unless they are thoroughly convinced that profits will be generated in the respective years of the investment.

Of course, convertible preferred stock can be converted to common stock and thereby obtain voting rights accordingly. This equity may be a little more palatable for investors who believe that the company has the propensity to generate profits, but wish to retain the contingent right to convert their preferred shareholder interest into common shareholder interest to make use of their voting rights to possibly affect change in company management if there is no return on their investment or the return on their investment has not met their expectations.

The second method of corporate finance consists of the sale of debt. Yes, it is possible for a shareholder in a corporation to own debt instead of equity. Ownership interest in debt owed by the corporation to an individual investor is called a debenture. Holders of debentures are paid before any equity holders are paid. Initial investors may want to consider loaning money to the company in contrast to owning an interest in the company. They would have a defined rate of return by virtue of the interest rate associated with the debt instrument. They could also manage the risks of their investment based upon a debt risk analysis as opposed to a thorough evaluation of the propensity of the equity investment to hold value throughout the existence of the business.

There are also hybrid forms of corporate finance that consist of both equity and debt characteristics. These include warrants, options, convertible debentures, debentures with warrants, and other derivatives.

A warrant is a document that guarantees that a person or entity has the right to purchase equity interest in a business at a specified price. The specified price is usually nominal as it relates to general market conditions. Warrants do not generally have a specific period of time that they must be exercised within.

An option is similar to a warrant. However, an option has a contingent interest in acquiring the rights in the agreement providing the option. The option provides the holder the right to purchase equity interests in the business at a specified price for a specific period of time. Therefore, an option does terminate after a certain period of time.

Convertible debentures give investors the opportunity to convert their debt instrument to an equity position. The terms of the conversion are negotiated between the corporation and the investor. The debt instrument could be converted into preferred or common stock, depending on the negotiated terms.

As with convertible preferred stock, if the debenture is converted to common stock, it would most likely include voting rights attributes. A debenture with a warrant is an instrument that provides for the conversion of the debt instrument into an equity instrument upon the occurrence of certain triggering factors as described in the terms of the debenture warrant documents.

In addition to the variety in the types of investment instruments that can be offered by a corporation, the corporation can be structured to allow for varying levels of investment interests. A corporation can split its equity structure into different classes and series. A class is an identifiable level of stock ownership such as Class A or Class B shareholders. A series is an identifiable level of stock ownership in a particular class. These equity structural divisions allow for a corporation to attribute certain rights to shareholders at varying levels and degrees. The series may also be indicative of the timing of the proposed sale of the various equity instruments.

The class and series designations can also apply to the structure of debt securities in a corporation. You could also see a combination of equity and debt securities in the corporate structure that are separated by class or series so that the rights of the various shareholders are defined with a greater degree of certainty.

Entrepreneurs should be familiar with these various forms of equity and debt instruments that can be used to capitalize a corporation with the sale of investment securities. It would benefit them in their dealings with prospective investors to have a diverse group of investment options that they could offer depending upon their circumstances. It would also help them:

(1) analyze and structure possible multi-entity structures,

(2) arrange deals with other companies that may affect the equity configuration of the business,

(3) or present various forms of equity as collateral in a secured transaction.

It is also essential that the entrepreneur understands the basic distinction between public corporations and privately held corporations. Privately held corporations are those corporations that are owned by a limited number of investors. Privately held corporations are entities whose investment securities are generally not required to be filed with the Securities and Exchange Commission. But the corporation is required to abide by all of the laws associated with securities regulation.

Public corporations are those entities that desire to sell investment securities to a large number of outside investors in an effort to capitalize the corporation. They are required to make periodic filings with the Securities and Exchange Commission. They are subject to an extremely intense regulatory environment that is designed to protect the investors.

A public corporation most often begins as a privately held corporation. The founders of the privately held corporation can make a decision to sell the investment securities to the public market to increase the amount of capital for the corporation. It is an expensive and demanding proposition, but, if handled properly, can reap great benefits for the growth and development of the corporation. A detailed discussion of the process of taking a company public is beyond the scope of this book. If you would like more information on this topic, I suggest that you obtain resources to acquire a basic background on the regulation of the securities markets. However, you should remember that you need very specialized experts to assist you in the process if you choose to pursue that form of financing.

Limited Liability Company

This form of business organization is capitalized much as a corporation. If you recall from the previous chapters, the limited liability company is best described as a hybrid between a partnership and a corporation. A limited liability company can use all forms of investment capital instruments that can be used in a corporate structure. The limited liability company can rely upon equity or debt securities or hybrid combinations of the two as well. The identification of the various instruments could differ depending upon the laws within the state jurisdiction in which it is formed. However, the approach and methods for financing the limited liability company should be the same as that of the corporation.

Business Capitalization

As you can see, there are many ways to capitalize a business. It is always best to consider all options available. However, you cannot choose from options that you do not know exist. Avail yourself to this and other information on corporate and business capitalization and finance. It is the foundation of your business infrastructure and your platform for business growth.

The Map to Entrepreneurship

Chapter 8

Commercial Finance

In contrast to equity and quasi-equity corporate financing associated with ownership in a business organization, businesses may also seek to obtain debt financing by borrowing funds from financial institutions or individuals to capitalize the business enterprise. This is generally referred to as commercial financing since it is designed to fund business operations in their quest to pursue commercial enterprise without the business directly allotting a significant amount of ownership in the business to the funding source. However, there are circumstances in which commercial financing could involve some form of an equity outlay. We will discuss such financing structures later in this chapter.

There are several different types of commercial finance alternatives. This area consists of various methods and mechanisms that are structured in a manner that represents the negotiated terms between the business and the financial institution depending upon several factors. We will discuss the basic considerations in commercial financing as well as evaluate the many different debt structures available to businesses.

There are many factors that lenders take into consideration when determining the availability, flexibility, cost, and terms of any financing arrangement with a business. A newly formed business may face greater obstacles in obtaining commercial financing than a more established business that has a financial history. Though there are substantial obstacles, those can be overcome at times based upon factors such as the financial stability of the owners of the business, the presence of a professional and practical business plan, and the willingness of the owners to guaranty the debt under the business loans.

> One of the reasons for establishing multi-entity structures is to leverage the assets and combined financial history of all entities operating under a parent organization.

For an entrepreneur, one of the reasons for establishing multi-entity structures is to leverage the assets and combined financial history of all entities operating under a parent organization. It may not only give the business an advantage in the combination of financial information, but it could give the lender a larger collateral base to consider in evaluating whether there is enough collateral to secure the loan. A business with multi-entity structures also possibly has greater flexibility in structuring loan transactions.

Here are some alternative structuring arrangements that could be used by multi-entity structures:

(1) All of the entities in the multi-entity structure could be co-borrowers in the loan transaction;

(2) One entity could be the borrower with the other entities acting in the capacity of guarantors for the loan;

(3) One entity could be the borrower while presenting its rights in the assets of the other entities as additional collateral to be security for repayment of the loan;

or

(4) Any other variation that would not be contrary to public policy or law that could meet the requirements of the lender.

Types of Business and Commercial Loans

The phrase commercial loan generally describes any loan structure that involves a lender loaning money to a person or entity for business purposes. However, there are several types of commercial loans that can be used by the lender to accommodate the needs of the business based upon its current circumstances. As you may guess, since a business goes through many phases of growth and development, a business may need to structure several different types of commercial loan arrangements throughout its existence.

■ Term Loans:

The most basic commercial loan is the term loan. This is a loan from a lender with a specified period of time for repayment. Short-term loans are those loans that customarily must be paid in their entirety within one year or less from their effective date. Bridge loans, also referred to as mezzanine financing, consists of loans extending between one and five years. Mezzanine financing is relied upon by businesses that are seeking to expand their operations or need funding to acquire another business operation. Long-term loans are most often described as those loans that must be paid in their entirety within any time period of five years or greater.

■ Revolving Line of Credit:

A revolving line of credit is almost self-identifying. It refers to a loan arrangement whereby the outstanding balance under a loan transaction revolves depending on the needs of the business during its course of operation. Revolving lines of credit are considered a popular form of financing for those businesses that are in need of periodic short-term financing.

Asset-Based Lending:

One category of loan transactions is often identified as asset-based lending. Asset-based lending primarily involves equipment and inventory financing. Asset-based lending transactions are unique in that they are based solely on the purchase of assets by the business for its operations. They may be short-term, mezzanine, or long-term arrangements. The term is conditioned upon the amount and type of assets purchased with the financed funds, the prospective depreciation of the assets, and the potential risks in maintaining the assets and their value. This type of loan structure may also include a revolving line of credit component, depending on the ability of the business to meet the requirements of the lender.

Accounts Receivable Financing:

Accounts receivable financing refers to the use of the accounts receivable of a business as collateral for financing the business operations. It is common for these arrangements to be designed to fund the working capital needs of the business when the accounts receivable of the business are slow in processing or the nature of the business causes a delay in the receipt of the business revenue.

These are complex business transactions since they involve a constantly evolving asset. Therefore, lenders will use specialists who are familiar with monitoring and auditing the accounts receivable of a business. The process for monitoring and auditing accounts receivable is extensive. Accordingly, accounts receivable financing involves higher than average interest rates and other fees and charges. It could be a costly form of business financing, but there are times when a business is left with no alternative.

■ Factoring:

Factoring is very similar to accounts receivable financing in that factoring involves the transfer of rights or interest in the accounts receivable of a business. However, factoring actually involves the purchase of accounts receivable by a financial institution or company. The lender thereby obtains all of the borrower's rights and interest in the accounts receivable that the lender purchases. The amount of funds received by the business from the lender for the purchase of its accounts receivable is used for working capital in the business operations.

■ Letters of Credit:

A letter of credit is an agreement made by a financial institution, such as a bank, to a customer. The agreement provides the business with the right to make demands for the lender to pay another party once the conditions set forth in the letter of credit have been met. A business arranges this type of transaction with a financial institution when the business desires for payment to another party to be subject to completion of an obligation by the other party before the payment is distributed.

The business must be creditworthy. It must also meet the criteria set by the financial institution for honoring the requested amount of credit for issuing the letter of credit. This form of financing is used frequently in import–export commercial transactions involving international trade and shipments.

■ Leasing:

Many businesses do not consider leasing to be a form of financing. However, leasing can be characterized as such, depending on the structure of the transaction between the parties arranging the leasing relationship. Leasing arrangements are most often associated with financing depreciable assets such as vehicles.

■ General Factors Affecting All Loan Structures:

By now, you should be aware that financial relationships for your business could be very diverse. The transactions encountered could also be as diverse as the proposed business relationships. This section is designed to give you a brief summary of many of the tools that are used in documenting financial transactions. I recommend that you use this knowledge of the various tools and resources in considering, handling, and structuring transactions. Hopefully, this chapter will assist you in that process.

■ Secured or Unsecured

One of the first issues for determination by the lender is whether the loan will be secured or unsecured. If the loan is to be secured, the lender will require you to place some form of property as collateral for the loan. This means that you give the lender the right to take possession of that certain property used as collateral upon any occurrence of default under a loan. If the loan is unsecured, there is no requirement for the borrower to use any of its property as collateral for the loan, and thus the borrower's property is not immediately accessible by the lender for collection upon default under the loan.

Most business loans will be secured unless there is a proven record of payment history by the business with the particular lender. The type of collateral required by a lender varies depending upon the type of loan and the type of business requesting the loan. The amount of the loan and the fair market value of the prospective collateral are also important considerations. It is also common for a lender to require a blanket lien on all of the assets of the business to serve as collateral for the loan if the relationship between the business and the lender is new.

■ Guarantor or Other Accommodating Party

Lenders may also request that the owners of the business guaranty the repayment of the debt under the business loan. This shows the lender that the owners of the business are as committed to the success of their business as the lender is committed to investing in the business's success. Under such circumstances, the person guarantees that he or she assumes personal responsibility for the debt upon the occurrence of any default under the loan agreements.

There are a couple of methods to accomplish this result. Individuals or other business entities can act as guarantors and thus guarantee the repayment of debt under the loan agreements. Another method involves including the individuals or other business entities as parties to the loan agreement documents and subsequently become jointly and severally liable for the debt incurred under the loan. The methods usually have the same net effect since the terms of the guaranty agreement generally require the guarantor to be jointly and severally liable for the debt under the loan. However, the guarantor can negotiate the terms of the guaranty agreement to be more flexible if there are other factors that give the lender a greater degree of confidence in the repayment ability of the business.

■ Terms of Payment

The term of the loan depends on the type of loan and the nature of the business receiving the loan. The payment terms are also based upon the same factors. Payment terms for term loans are often based on monthly payment schedules. Of course, there could be many variations. There are also balloon payment structures available that involve payments of interest only throughout the term of the loan and a final lump sum payment upon maturity of the loan. The structure of payment terms is almost always negotiable on a case-by-case basis with the lender.

■ Interest Rates

The interest rate in business loan transactions can be determined based on the costs of funds for the lender or some other similar basis. The lender has a profit margin that it seeks to obtain, just as any other business. The lender's profit margin must also factor in the risks associated with each individual loan with each borrower. This is why the lender seeks to use as many tools as possible to mitigate its risks. By doing so, the lender is able to remain competitive with other lenders by offering competitive interest rates and keeping some flexibility with its margin requirements. The fluctuations in the federally designated rate of interest also cause changes in the cost of money for the lender. Therefore, it would be prudent to research the current economic conditions in financial markets, including the existing prime rate of interest, when seeking a lender.

Documentation of the Loan Transaction:

■ Loan Agreement

The loan agreement is the primary document in the loan transaction. This agreement details the rights and obligations of each of the parties to the loan transaction. The lender includes all provisions that it believes to be pertinent in its efforts to protect its interests under the lending arrangement. Many of the items we previously discussed are covered in this agreement such as the amount of the loan, terms of payment, the security interests associated with the lending arrangement (collateral required to be presented by the borrower to support repayment of the loan), the conditions of the loan, representations and warranties by the parties, and other relevant provisions.

■ Promissory Note

The promissory note can be considered a negotiable instrument in many cases. Many new entrepreneurs do not realize that a promissory note can be as negotiable as cash or a check if the note meets the specific requirements for negotiability. It is prepared to document the ownership of a debt. The promissory note symbolizes the lender's rights to repayment of the debt under a loan the lender has made to a borrower. The specific terms of repayment and conditions of repayment are also included in many promissory notes. These promissory notes are usually transferable for the lender. That is why it is possible that a lender could assign your loan to other lenders with the same terms and conditions as long as it is deemed to be assignable in the loan agreement documents as well as the promissory note.

■ Guaranty Agreement

This is the agreement signed by a guarantor, usually one or more of the owners of a business, to guarantee repayment of the debt under the loan to the business. The agreements are drafted in such a way that the guarantor assumes all contingent responsibility for the repayment of the loan. However, after the business has developed a successful payment history and established itself as a profitable venture, the lender will sometimes consider releasing the guarantor from the obligations under the guaranty agreement.

> A lender must comply with specific legal requirements to acquire and maintain security interests in the property of the borrower.

■ Security Agreements

A lender must comply with specific legal requirements to acquire and maintain security interests in the property of the borrower. I will not delineate all of the details of the legal requirements, but you should be aware that lenders must not only have your agreement to provide a security interest in the property, but they must perfect the security interests agreed upon in the security agreements. The procedure for perfection of security interests depends on the type of property delivered as collateral, the location of the property, and a stringent framework of rules under the Uniform Commercial Code that must be followed.

Security agreements are used if the secured transaction provisions in the loan agreement do not sufficiently address the matters in connection with the collateral presented as security for the loan. Sometimes they are used to create distinct obligations for the borrower and the lender in relation to the collateral presented for the loan.

Security agreements are also used to document unique forms of security interest. This is often done when there is a pledge of the issued and outstanding stock of the corporation in addition to the delivery of other property in connection with the security interest for the loan. In these situations, the transaction would include a stock pledge agreement for all shareholders presenting their shares of stock in the corporation as collateral for the loan as well as a security agreement for other assets of the corporation that the parties desire to be presented as collateral for the loan.

The security agreement usually includes, at a minimum, the following:

(1)   a detailed description of the property presented as collateral for the loan,

(2) provisions describing the responsibilities of the lender in acquiring, perfecting, and maintaining its security interest in the property, and

(3) provisions explaining the procedures for a lender in exercising it rights to take full possession of the collateral upon an occurrence of default under the loan.

■ Financing Statements

Financing statements are forms that are filed with the state regulatory bodies to perfect security interests in certain forms of property of a debtor. Financing forms are not applicable to all types of property. You should just be aware that this is a document you may be required to sign as a business representative in connection with other loan transaction documents.

■ Warrants

A warrant may also be executed for the benefit of a lender in certain circumstances. As previously discussed, a warrant is a type of equity interest in the business. A warrant is used in lending transactions to provide the lender with an asset that may be leveraged when financing the existing or proposed business venture in spite of the extremely high risk associated with the venture. An entrepreneur should be cautious in agreeing to such arrangements unless he or she believes that the business venture could be a very risky proposition from a lender's perspective and a less intrusive financial relationship is not available.

A warrant is also a popular legal tool used in mezzanine financing and other forms of long-term financing. Of course, you should proceed with caution even under these circumstances. It is understandable that additional financing may be needed for increased growth and development, but you must remember that a warrant gives an equity interest to an outside entity regardless of how nominal it may seem at the time. You should first ask the question, "Is the lender really wanting to protect itself from risk or is it simply seeking an extraordinary return on investment?"

■ Options

These arrangements should also be handled with caution in the context of using options in financial transactions with lenders. If a lender desires to participate in the potential success of the business, the lender may not consider the business to be as risky as you would assume. If that is the case, then the option to obtain equity interest may not be justifiable to mitigate risks under the lending relationship.

■ Subordination Agreements

In some cases, there may be a need for more than one lender to serve the financial needs of the business. The business may have an existing lending relationship whereby the lender seeks to maintain its position as the senior lender. On the other hand, a new lender may be willing to provide a larger loan amount with better terms and thus request that the existing lender subordinate its rights with the debtor in order to protect its interests in assuming a greater degree of risks. In either case, the lender seeking to maintain its senior position will require the other lenders to subordinate their rights under their loan agreements to the rights of its loan agreements. These contractual arrangements are called subordination agreements.

The debtor as well as all lenders that are subordinating their rights under their loan documents must be parties to the subordination agreements. There is a tremendous amount of negotiation involved in dealing with these types of lending transactions.

■ Intercreditor Agreements

Intercreditor Agreements are separate agreements between lenders that designate their rights and obligations between themselves in relation to specific loan transactions with the same debtor. These agreements could designate the respective security interests to be shared by the lenders or establish differing priorities in relation to their rights with a common debtor. Unlike subordination agreements, these agreements could be separately negotiated between the lenders without a tremendous amount of involvement from the debtor. However, it is very important to understand the terms of these agreements because they affect your business's relationships with the various lenders.

■ Corporate Resolutions

Corporate resolutions are required to represent and warrant that the appropriate officers of the business have the authority to act on behalf of the business entity. There may be other resolutions required as well. The company may be required to acknowledge such items as the following:

(1) the solvency of the business,

(2) confirmation of the veracity and accuracy of the representations made under the agreements,

(3) confirmation of meeting conditions for the loans, and

(4) other matters confirming the legitimacy of the proposed financial relationship.

■ The Process

As a former General Counsel to a finance company, I am familiar with the process most lenders use to determine the viability of entering into a financial arrangement with a business. The process most often begins with the business owner or entrepreneur completing an application on behalf of the business to finance the business operations. The application also requires submission of various documents for the lender to review, along with the information contained in the application responses. The company's business plan is usually reviewed in connection with the loan application documents as well.

The next step involves the review of the prospective borrower's application and document submissions by the lender's loan processors. The well-established lender will generally have an internal due diligence checklist of the information and documentation that is required to satisfy the requirements for each applicable loan requested. The loan processor contacts the representatives of the business if more information and/or documentation are required.

Once the loan processor is satisfied that all of the information has been obtained from the business applicant, a completed file is organized and submitted to a loan or credit committee for review. The committee reviews the requests for financing and determines the criteria that should be used to make a decision on each respective applicant. The committee will often determine the appropriate loan approval for the applicant.

After loan approval, a loan sales representative will usually prepare and submit a proposal to the business owner with the proposed terms of the financing relationship. The document that is presented from the lender with the proposed terms is often referred to as the "term sheet."

The term sheet is not generally a contractual document. However, it will present the basic lender requirements for the borrowers. A discussion of the various types of agreements that you are likely to encounter when conducting loan transactions was presented in the previous section of this chapter.

Though not comprehensive, the term sheet will set forth, at a minimum, the following:

(a) the amount of the loan approval,

(b) the time period for repayment of the loan,

(c) the rate of interest to be charged for the loan,

(d) other fees and charges imposed by the lender in connection with the loan arrangement,

(e) a list of any collateral that may be required to secure repayment of the loan,

(f) a list of guarantors or other accommodating parties that may be required to guaranty repayment of the loan,

(g) representations and warranties required from the borrowers, and

(h) other special conditions that are a part of the loan relationship.

After the term sheet is presented, the business borrowers have the opportunity to review the proposed terms, respond with any requested changes to the terms, notify the lender of which obligations and requirements that the business will be unable to satisfy, and suggest any alternative methods of handling the lender's concerns. Remember that the lender's concern about the ability of the business to repay the debt is the key element for decisions on the terms proposed by the lender to the business. Therefore, it is in the business's best interest to take measures to give the lender comfort in its ability to repay the debt in a timely manner.

After the lender and borrowers have agreed upon the terms specified in the term sheet, the parties begin negotiating the terms of the loan documents applicable to the contemplated business arrangement between them. There are several types of agreements that could be included in the loan transaction documents, as was discussed earlier in this chapter. Once the applicable loan documents are finalized and fully signed by the appropriate parties, the lender appoints an account manager or other representatives to manage the loan accounts for the business borrowers. The account managers or account representatives service the accounts based upon the terms of loan documents.

Most lenders will audit the accounts on a periodic basis. There may also be occasions that require the lender and borrowers to adjust the terms of the loan arrangement to meet the changing conditions or needs of the business. These changes are negotiated with each borrower's circumstances being taken into consideration. Such changes are generally made only at the discretion of the lender.

It may be essential for a business to obtain commercial financing. However, it is also essential that the business representatives have a basic understanding of the commercial finance framework. You may use such information to position your business to act in its best interest in all commercial finance transactions. Position your business for growth and success.

> It may be essential for a business to obtain commercial financing. However, it is also essential that the business representative have a basic understanding of the commercial finance framework.

Chapter 9

Commercial Transactions

I describe all commercial transactions as transactions between individuals or entities that are designed to fulfill a commercial purpose. This business category generally consists of written contractual agreements whereby parties are attempting to memorialize the structure and function of their relationships with other businesses and individuals. This section is applicable to many other chapters in this book because it involves any transaction in which a contractual agreement of any kind is contemplated for a commercial business purpose.

The reason that I included this chapter with such broad subject matter is to impress upon you the importance of forming binding contractual relationships and comprehending the basic methods and reasons for entering into such business relationships. The types of transactions and agreements discussed in this chapter concern relationships that often directly affect day-to-day operations of a business. I have not included the information that is covered more thoroughly in other chapters. Transactions involving equity-based agreements between owners of separate businesses are discussed in the chapter titled "corporate transactions." Commercial financial transactions are discussed in greater detail in the chapter titled "commercial finance."

I believe that an entrepreneur should always view commercial transactions from the perspective of having a method of protecting the rights of the business. Properly documenting business relationships should not be viewed as an inconvenience but rather as value-added methods to protect and increase the assets of the business organization. This chapter is designed to summarize what I believe to be some of the most important subject matter areas for transactions that are most vital to continuity of business operations and protecting the rights of the business.

General Factors for All Commercial Transactions

There are contractual issues that are pertinent to any commercial transaction. These and many more issues that evolve from these transactions are very intricate. Therefore, you should always seek legal counsel to ensure that all of the legal nuances are addressed. As with the other sections of this book, this section is only designed to give you basic familiarity with the concepts associated with commercial transactions so that the terminology will not seem foreign to you when you establish and manage the operations of your business.

I believe there is a misconception among beginning entrepreneurs that any agreement made between two individuals or entities is considered a contractual agreement. However, it is important for you to know that every proposed contractual arrangement must have specific elements in order to be enforceable as a binding contractual agreement.

The basic elements of a contract are as follows:

(1)　An offer is made by one party;

(2)　There is an acceptance of the offer made by the other parties;

(3)　There is adequate consideration, which consists of a mutual bargained exchange of something of value between the parties; and

(4)　There is mutual assent and a meeting of the minds between the parties whereby all parties to the agreement are in consistent agreement with the terms of the arrangement whereby there is a bargained-for exchange. However, there are also other circumstances whereby an agreement could be binding without all of the elements being met.

One thing you should always remember is that a promise from someone else to do something does not automatically make the promise a binding contractual agreement. It could possibly be an illusory promise whereby one party promises to do something and the other does not agree to do anything in consideration for the promise. Such an arrangement does not create a contractual relationship. It would be advisable to evaluate every contractual relationship to ensure that the transaction will be enforceable as it is written.

All contractual agreements should be prepared with the least amount of ambiguity as possible. A written contractual agreement is simply a formalized documentation of the mutual understanding of parties based upon a bargained-for exchange between the parties.

■ Terms and Conditions

The most important aspect to any contractual agreement is the description of the services to be performed or the products to be sold. Each contract should thoroughly describe the reasoning for the parties to enter into the agreement and accurately present the bargained-for exchange that is the basis for the contractual arrangement.

Equally as important is a specification of the conditions under which the services or products are to be delivered. If there are general or special requirements associated with the subject matter of the agreement, these items most likely would be set forth under the terms and conditions section of the agreement.

It is important for business representatives to thoroughly understand the economic implications of the terms described in the agreement. If the language seems a bit confusing, it could be helpful to chart the economic components in a separate table of calculations or include examples in the provisions and incorporate the chart, table, or examples into the terms of the agreement to alleviate any confusion or ambiguity and ensure the mutual understanding of the financial and economic components of the agreement.

> **I**t is important for business representatives to thoroughly understand the economic implications of the terms described in the agreement.

■ Representations and Warranties

Each party in a contractual agreement desires to have an assurance of certain expectations that it has of the other parties prior to entering into an agreement. The preliminary assurances and expectations are normally incorporated into the representations and warranties section of contractual agreements. Though many people perceive these provisions to be standard boilerplate language, there could be some very significant guarantees incorporated into the contents.

Express warranties are those that are expressly stated in the contract as warranties being made by one party to the other for the services being performed. Implied warranties are those warranties that exist under the precedence of current law whether or not they are expressly stated in the agreement. Implied warranties can be waived in a contract if the waivers are conspicuously set forth in the contract and all other pertinent conditions are met for the implied warranties to be waived.

Some of the most common representation and warranty provisions include the following:

(1) acknowledgment that the party has the legal right to enter into the agreement,

(2) acknowledgments that the party is appropriately organized in the business entity structure identified,

(3) covenant that the party will operate in accordance with all federal and state laws at all times throughout the term of the agreement, and

(4) representation that the agreement will not violate the terms or conditions of any other agreement between the business organization and a third party.

■ Uniform Commercial Code Implications

The Uniform Commercial Code is a broad conglomeration of rules related to commercial transactions that is generally accepted by most state jurisdictions; its concepts are consequently codified into their statutes. There are specific rules associated with the sales of goods between merchants as that term is defined in the rules. For example, there is a specific requirement that contracts for the sale of goods between merchants contain conspicuously printed language in order for any waivers of implied or expressed warranties to be effective. There are also rules that are pertinent to general contract interpretation and performance. Moreover, there is some codification related to service agreements in many statutes.

■ Indemnification

Indemnification has become an essential provision for almost every contractual relationship. The language in this provision requires that one party to the agreement will release and hold harmless the other parties from any and all liabilities that may be incurred as a result of the actions of those parties. In other words, indemnification requires one party to accept full responsibility for its actions or omissions and usually requires it to defend the other parties if claims are brought against them by a third party for such actions or omissions.

These provisions generally require an organization to release the other parties from any actions or omissions of the organization so designated as well as hold the other parties harmless from claims asserted against them. I often consider indemnity provisions to be what I call contractual based insurance or risk management. Indemnification places all liabilities and responsibilities on the respective parties. If you are asked to sign an agreement with such a provision, be careful in agreeing to indemnify all claims and liabilities regardless of the source of the claims. I generally try to limit indemnification solely to the acts or omissions of my organization if it is requested.

◼ Force Majeure Provisions

A force majeure provision is designed to excuse the performance of one or more parties in an agreement as a result of the occurrence of events beyond the control of the parties. Though these types of provisions are often overlooked as boilerplate, they are very important in time-sensitive contractual arrangements as well as those contractual relationships with a certain date or dates of performance. Force majeure provisions are particularly important in service contracts.

◼ Choice of Law Provisions

It is common for most contractual agreements to have a provision identifying the appropriate state law that will be applicable to determine issues under the contract. These provisions may also designate the state and local venue in which any dispute related action is required to take place. This could become a hot topic for negotiation for parties that reside in two different state jurisdictions. However, in my opinion, it is worth negotiating the matter since the cost of civil litigation in a foreign jurisdiction could be unmanageable.

■ Alternative Dispute Resolution

Contractual provisions mandating that all disputes between the parties be resolved in some form of alternative dispute resolution as opposed to resolution in a civil litigation proceeding in a court of law have become standard in many contractual arrangements. The most popular forms of alternative dispute resolution are mediation and arbitration. Arbitration provisions usually specify that any arbitration proceeding between the parties will be conducted in accordance with the rules promulgated by the American Arbitration Association. Other alternative dispute resolution procedures may be used. I believe the most important issue to remember in this area is that the rules, procedures, and processes to be followed for such proceedings should be specifically described or referenced in this provision of the contractual agreement.

Common Types of Commercial Transactions

■ Real Estate Transactions

It is inevitable that every business entity will need to be involved in some form of real estate transaction at some point throughout its existence. Small start-up companies will likely begin their experiences by negotiating leasehold arrangements for the business location. This could include office leases, warehouse leases, or possibly shopping center leases. Each form of lease has differentiating features.

Other companies may seek to acquire real estate with existing improvements on the property. This type of purchase of real estate involves the transfer of real property interests from one property owner to an individual or entity. There are also other business entities that may desire to acquire raw land or real property in new real estate developments in order to begin construction projects if they desire to construct their own facilities. There are many variations to real estate transactions, but the form of transactions in real estate usually follow a progression that tracks the growth and development of the business organization.

Any and all contractual agreements in real estate transactions must be in writing. The legal community refers to this requirement as the statute of frauds. It was determined that there was a need to ensure that all real estate transactions are adequately documented as well as any other contractual relationship that is not performable within the term of one year. Of course, as discussed previously, it is my opinion that all contractual agreements should be in writing regardless of the circumstances.

■ Service Agreements

A distinction can be made between agreements related to the provision of services and agreements made in connection with the sales of goods. There are matters that are significant to service agreements that are not as applicable to sales of products.

Service agreements should adequately describe the services being provided by the service provider. Service agreements should also describe the compensation structure and the time period for the provision of services. There should be a standard of satisfactory performance established in the agreement.

It may be necessary to require the service provider to meet special conditions of performance. These special conditions could be necessary to establish a prerequisite before performance is required by another party. This type of condition is often referred to as a condition precedent. Conditions may also be necessary for the parties to identify matters that are required to be met after a certain performance requirement has been completed. This type of condition is referred to as a condition subsequent.

One goal in structuring service agreement arrangements is to ensure that the risks are mitigated as much as possible. Therefore, I also include indemnity provisions and insurance requirements for most service agreements. The indemnity requires the other party defend you and hold you harmless from any liabilities associated with the other parties actions or omissions. Requiring the other party to maintain a certain amount of insurance protection will also give you the comfort of knowing that there is some form of protection available to cover any of those claims that are subject to indemnification.

Representations and warranties are also important provisions under service contracts. This is surely the case if one or more parties require warranties. These provisions are also significant in service agreements if any warranties are specifically waived. The law recognizes both express and implied warranties.

If your industry requires certain licensing or certification for you to maintain with service providers, you may want to look for provisions that mandate that the service provider represents and warrants its compliance with the requisite licensing or certification standards. This is applicable when the state jurisdiction requires certain services providers to meet certain licensing requirements in order to provide services so that the public interest is protected.

Specific standards of conduct may also be considered for inclusion in the agreement. If there is a certain moral or other underlying standard that must be maintained in the relationship between the service provider and the client, there are provisions that can be inserted that could address those exceptional standards. This type of provision is often included in service agreements if one party seeks to protect its reputation from being tarnished by external factors associated with a third-party contractual arrangement.

■ Sales Agreements

The general contract provision issues also apply to contracts for the sale of goods. On the other hand, agreements made in relation to the sales of goods have different issues that are more applicable to their arrangements. There is also a regulatory framework under the Uniform Commercial Code that specifically applies to sales of goods between merchants. Of course, all sale of goods transactions may also have important considerations. Issues associated with sales of goods include representations and warranties, delivery requirements, description of goods, payment obligations, assumption of risks, and product liability. Agreements associated with the sale of goods must also be established in accordance with the industry standards and nature of the products being sold.

■ Manufacturing Agreements

As you are probably aware, the methods chosen to manufacture various products and goods can vary from industry to industry. As a result, manufacturing agreements are designed to be industry specific. The primary business for a manufacturer is to produce goods in a systematic manner through process designs that add efficiency and productivity for the benefit of the customer company. Some companies that produce goods may wish to develop their own manufacturing facilities in an effort to have complete control over the manufacturing process. However, it generally requires a tremendous amount of capital for a company to have the financial strength to develop those facilities and support the day-to-day operations of the business.

■ Distribution Agreements

Companies that desire to establish a distribution process and network through outside vendors and not from their own internal business operations may enter into distribution agreements. It could be more economically feasible to hire outside vendors for this service if the vendor's primary business function is to provide distribution services, and they have an infrastructure assembled that can distribute or accommodate an enormous volume of products in a more efficient manner and at a lower cost than the company could do within its internal operations.

There are several matters that should be considered in these types of business arrangements, such as the following:

(1) deciding whether the distributor will be manufacturing and distributing the products or simply providing distribution and logistical services,

(2) determination of who owns intellectual property rights for the products to be distributed,

(3) the extent, if any, that intellectual property rights will be transferred to the distributor,

(4) the compensation percentages to the distributor,

(5) the formula for calculating the compensation percentages such as determining whether it will be based upon gross or net revenues, and

(6) if based upon net revenues, whether there are sufficient covenants and obligations in the agreement that make the distributor accountable for expenditures or to place limitations on expenditures. This list is certainly not comprehensive, but it should give you an idea of the matters that should be considered.

Distribution arrangements can definitely affect the bottom line of a company and should be analyzed and negotiated thoroughly. However, if structured properly, they can be extremely beneficial in helping a company reach its goals of growth and economic success.

■ Transactions Involving Intellectual Property

Intellectual property is a very specialized area. In fact, many people do not realize that patent attorneys must complete a separate admissions process before being admitted to practice before the United States Patent and Trademark Office. All areas of intellectual property can be intricate and complicated. It can also be one of the most important areas for creating value in the business enterprise. For these reasons, I always recommend that a business entity appropriately establish and protect its rights to its intellectual property at the early stages of business planning and development. It is also best to obtain the assistance of a professional who specializes in such areas when doing so.

> All areas of intellectual property can be intricate and complicated. It can also be one of the most important areas for creating value in the enterprise business.

■ Copyrights, Patents, Trademarks, and Trade Names

Most business ventures have some form of assets that are intangible but add the most significant value to the business. This could be a branding concept, a uniquely identifiable name or phrase, a newly developed process or method for product development or services, a new technological concept, or a new invention. The legal rights to all of these and other significant marketing and product assets must be established and protected by the business that seeks to claim an interest in owning them. The method for claiming those legal rights depends upon the nature of the property being protected.

Any rights to be claimed to a new invention must be assigned and licensed to the owner by the United States Patent and Trademark Office. The claiming owner must file an application for patent with the United States Patent and Trademark Office in order to obtain legal rights to claim the invention or new product.

If a company desires to protect its use of a particular name, logo, or other identifiable object, the company must appropriately establish its rights to claim ownership of the trade name or trademark. Applications for protection of rights in these forms of intellectual property can also be filed with the United States Patent and Trademark Office. However, there are other considerations in obtaining such rights such as the timing of usage and method of usage of the name or object.

Copyright interests apply to certain works or materials that have been created and for which ownership is claimed. This right prevents another party from reproducing any works or materials that are claimed as another party's intellectual property. There is a separate government agency that regulates copyright registration. The United States Copyright Office handles copyright registration. Though copyright registration is not required to claim such rights in materials, I always recommend that entrepreneurs avail themselves to the protection afforded under copyright registration. This protection of rights could prove to be invaluable to your company's assets.

■ Licensing

Licensing simply involves the transfer of limited rights to the use of intellectual property from one party to another. Licensing generally does not involve the absolute transfer of rights to the property. Licensing agreements are usually very detailed documents that contain several limitations and responsibilities associated with the rights of the party to use the intellectual property. These agreements are very prevalent with technology-based companies in association with software and other forms of technology. Licensing agreements are also commonly used in the entertainment industry.

■ Nondisclosure and Confidentiality Agreements

I believe nondisclosure and confidentiality agreements are essential for any business enterprise to use in all of its external business affairs. A good practice for entrepreneurs is to require any person who will be provided access to your business ideas and business plans who are not associated with the business entity to sign a nondisclosure and confidentiality agreement before obtaining the information.

An entrepreneur should consider that most transactions involving the transfer of financial information, including commercial financing arrangements, should include a nondisclosure and confidentiality agreement during the phases of due diligence and review. If you decide not to proceed with the transaction or to approach another financial institution, you do not want any confidential information disclosed to other third parties without your consent.

These types of agreements are also important when companies are considering a merger or acquisition. Mergers and acquisitions also involve a process of due diligence among the parties. The due diligence process includes the exchange of proprietary information from one party to the other in consideration of the proposed transaction. However, the parties must protect the information that is disclosed in case the transaction is not consummated. Therefore, rarely are such transactions entered into without the parties executing a nondisclosure and confidentiality agreement prior to the due diligence phase.

■ Employment Agreements

Most states have employment at-will statutes that allow for an employee to be terminated by an employer with or without cause. Therefore, employment agreements are most often used only to document special employment relationships. However, it is also advisable to include confidentiality and nondisclosure agreements in any employment documentation package. This is especially true for businesses where employees may be able to access confidential or proprietary information.

Chapter 10

Commercial and Business Disputes

It is a difficult truth to accept, but it is almost inevitable that disputes may arise in your business ventures. You should work diligently to design a plan that could prevent and/or mitigate the number and effect of such disputes. But that does not guarantee that you will never have a dispute-related matter to address in your business.

> **It is a difficult truth to accept, but it is almost inevitable that disputes may arise in your business ventures.**

It is certainly in the best interest of entrepreneurs to acquire and maintain an awareness of the various dispute-related matters that could affect the business. When most laypersons consider business disputes, they most often think of contractual disputes. However, contractual disputes are only one category of claims that could be made against the business. Though many claims could be related to contractual issues, there are several types of claims that could be made

> **It is certainly in the best interest of entrepreneurs to acquire and maintain an awareness of the various dispute-related matters that could affect the business.**

against a business that have no connection to a contractual agreement.

I would like for you to become somewhat familiar with some of the most common issues and claims that could be prevalent in commercial and business disputes. This is not a comprehensive overview, but again it is to provide you with information that you could use to intelligently discuss such concerns with a legal professional or possibly resolve the issues with the other parties by having a better understanding of the issues surrounding the disputes.

Contract-Related Disputes

Obviously, the number one category in the area of business disputes is most often claims for breach of contract. These claims are initiated by an allegation that at least one party to a contractual agreement has violated the terms of the agreement and consequently caused damages or losses to one or more of the other parties to the contractual agreement.

In order to establish such a claim, the complaining party must first establish that a contractual agreement exists between the parties. I will not bore you with a discussion of the elements required to substantiate a legally enforceable contractual relationship. However, you should be aware that a valid contract is required for any party to state a claim for breach of contract.

Many entrepreneurs without a legal background do not realize that there are quasi-contractual claims that can be asserted as well.

Generally, these claims do not require a legally enforceable agreement in order to be asserted. Such claims most likely occur where one party alleges that a party has suffered some form of damage or loss based upon a detrimental reliance on the acts of another party. There are several specific elements that must be proven to make such a claim, but such claims do exist.

Tort-Related Disputes

If you are like I was before I attended law school, you should be asking yourself the question, what in the world is a tort? Well, without going into an in-depth legal analysis, I would describe it as an act or omission by one party that causes harm to another party as a result of a breach of some duty owed by the party causing the harm.

An example that should be familiar to all of us is that of personal injury claims by a person injured in a car accident. Just as individuals owe a duty to one another to act or restrain from acting under certain situations based upon statutory, regulatory, or other legal authority, businesses also owe certain duties to other businesses and individuals. Therefore, you should be aware of some of the issues that could result in liability to your company if you do not handle them appropriately.

■ Interference with Contractual Relations

Tortious interference with contractual relations is a tort that evolves from one business inappropriately interfering with a contractual relationship between two or more other companies. Generally, in order for this type of claim to be asserted, there must be knowledge of an existing contractual relationship between two or more parties and interference by another party. A claimant must also show that the breach of the existing contractual agreement was proximately caused by the interference of another party.

The most important fact to recognize is that it could be unlawful for your business to interfere with an existing contractual relationship between two or more other parties. Respectively, it could also be unlawful for another party to interfere with an existing contractual relationship between your company and other parties. Therefore, your company's representatives must be very careful in how they handle existing contractual relationships with businesses representatives from other companies.

■ Interference with Prospective Contractual Relations

Interference with prospective contractual relations is a claim that is very similar to that of tortuous interference with contractual relations. There must be knowledge of a prospective contractual arrangement being considered by two or more parties and the intent of another party to interfere with that prospective contractual arrangement before the arrangement has been consummated into a contract. If the interference or other wrongful act of a party was the proximate cause of the prospective contractual arrangement failing to be consummated into a contract and a contract would have otherwise been executed and performed, then there may be a possible claim asserted for interference with prospective contractual relations.

As you can see, there are claims that may be asserted even in the absence of an existing contractual relationship between two or more parties. In addition to the causes of action described above, there are other possible claims that are available for similar circumstances and unethical business activities. Other available claims include negligent interference with contractual relations, intentional infliction of emotional distress, negligent infliction of emotional distress, and invasion of privacy.

It would be prudent for every entrepreneur to understand that the aforementioned circumstances and issues should be considered in all basic business negotiations and strategic development discussions. In the planning and strategic business development process, the company should implement and enforce general business policies that prohibit any form of unethical negotiations or any other form of business communication that could result in claims being asserted against the business.

■ Civil Conspiracy

In addition to the tortuous interference claims that may evolve from unethical business behavior, there is another claim that may evolve from unethical business behavior that involves the wrongful act of two or more parties in cooperation with each other. Civil conspiracy is basically the agreement between two or more entities to unlawfully harm other parties. These types of claims are often more difficult to prove because they involve the wrongful actions of more than one party with one common wrongful agenda. However, you should be aware that such claims do exist and that conspiracy is not limited to criminal circumstances.

■ Business Defamation

Business defamation consists of methods that wrongfully seek to destroy the reputation of a business. Intentional disparagement of the business is meant to cause damage to the economic interests of a company under these scenarios. Such claims arise when a party publishes false information to a third party, causing an actual economic loss to another party. There is also a claim related to business defamation called trade libel. Trade libel is viable when a party disparages the goods and services of a company as opposed to the reputation of the company. Of course, either form of defamation or disparagement of another business should be prohibited by your company's policies at all times. You should also note that these claims may be available to you if a company or individual seeks to disparage your business wrongfully.

■ Fraud

The claim of fraud is in a category all its own. Fraud can range from deceptive activities among business owners to deceptive activities between a business and government agencies. In my opinion, the basis of fraud is deception. Whenever there are scenarios presented in which there is some form of deception occurring between two or more parties, it is very possible that there is some form of fraud involved in the scenario. These claims also involve harm or damages sustained as a result of a detrimental reliance on the representations or omissions of another party.

■Civil Litigation

Civil litigation is the legal process that involves the resolution of disputes between two or more parties through courts of law. Civil litigation has a broad meaning in the legal context, but for the purpose of your enlightenment you should know that any court proceeding to address disputes between two or more businesses is generally handled through civil litigation.

> Civil litigation is the legal process that involves the resolution of disputes between two or more parties through courts of law.

First and foremost, any company or individual that encounters a dispute or possible dispute with another party should consult with an attorney. Preferably, it should be an attorney who specializes in civil litigation, and if there are business issues involved, he or she should have business litigation experience.

The civil litigation process usually begins with one party determining his or her rights under the law, both state and federal. In reviewing their rights under the law, the parties and their legal counsel will determine if they have potential claims or causes of action that apply to the particular facts presented in the dispute. They will also consider if there are defenses available to possible claims that could be alleged by another party. If there are claims that can be asserted, the legal counsel will draft and file a petition or complaint with the court that has proper jurisdiction to handle the disputed matters.

After a petition or complaint is filed, the defending party will have a certain amount of time to respond to the petition or complaint with an answer to the claims made by the claimant. These documents that designate the claims and defenses of the parties to the dispute are often referred to as the pleadings.

The parties are then allowed the opportunity to inquire and request information from the other party that is relevant to the dispute in accordance with civil procedure rules of the state and court of jurisdiction and the state and/or federal law that is applicable to the case. This phase is referred to as the discovery phase of civil litigation, and generally extends for the longest period of time and can be a very costly process. The most common forms of discovery are interrogatories, requests for admission, requests for production, and depositions.

Interrogatories are direct questions that are to be answered by the other party. Requests for admission are written requests for the other party to admit to certain facts. Requests for production are requests for the other party to deliver requested documents. Depositions consist of the direct questioning and testimony of particular witnesses that is recorded with the witnesses under oath. Of course, you should always remember that all of the discovery requests and responses to discovery are based upon intricate sets of rules and are subject to many limitations.

The discovery process could extend throughout the litigation process until the date of trial. The process is designed to give the parties the information needed to prepare for a trial where the disputed matters can be presented to the judge or a jury for a decision to be made based upon the presented facts.

Civil litigation can be a lengthy and expensive process for dispute resolution. Civil litigation is also an extremely time consuming endeavor for the legal counsel and the individual representatives involved in the civil litigation process. Therefore, it is

> Civil litigation can be a lengthy and expensive process for dispute resolution.

imperative that a business professional perform a true cost/benefit analysis when making a decision to pursue civil litigation to resolve disputes. In my experience, civil litigation is a difficult process for all parties involved. Consequently, many businesses now require that alternative dispute resolution provisions be inserted into agreements and thereby agreeing to eliminate the civil litigation process as an option.

■ Alternative Dispute Resolution

Forms of alternative dispute resolution include mediation, arbitration, and negotiation. Yes, I did include negotiation as an alternative dispute resolution tool. Most of us do not think of negotiation as a means to resolve disputes. It is most often discussed when parties desire to work through the terms of a prospective business relationship. However, negotiation can also be a powerful tool to work through the issues involved in a subsequent dispute between the parties. Of course, the only way for negotiation to be effective under such circumstances is for all parties to be voluntarily willing to discuss matters in a productive manner. Negotiation does not generally involve the input of a third party unless one party desires expert consultation.

Mediation is the process of resolution that requires a third party to serve as a mediator between the disputing parties. The mediator is a neutral person who must be objective throughout the resolution process. It is not the duty of the mediator to determine the resolution of the matter. The mediator is to only facilitate discussions between the parties to encourage them to resolve the matter on their own terms. If an agreement is not reached in the mediation process, the mediator has no power to force an agreement or to make a decision for the parties.

Arbitration, on the other hand, is the alternative dispute resolution tool that most business representatives are the most familiar with applying to their business disputes. This is a result of the overwhelming demand for arbitration provisions to be incorporated into many contractual agreements. Arbitration does involve a third-party decision-maker who renders a decision on the disputed issues. The arbitration process is generally less time intensive and has less formality than civil litigation. Arbitration is also more economically feasible than the civil litigation process. The parties to an agreement will usually designate the method for the arbitration as well as the rules that would apply to any arbitration proceedings. It is common to see provisions in contractual agreements requiring that all arbitration proceedings be conducted in accordance with the rules promulgated by the American Arbitration Association.

Risk Management and Asset Protection

Every entrepreneur should prepare to minimize the risks of loss resulting from regular business operations as well as the risks associated with potential disputes. Each business should be insured against certain risks. However, it is almost impossible for a business to obtain insurance protection for every potential matter that could develop during its business operations. Therefore, it would be in the best interest of each entrepreneur to take steps to protect the assets of the businesses as well as his or her personal assets as much as possible.

■ Insurance Protection

Obtaining adequate insurance protection to insure against potential liabilities that could be sustained by the business can mitigate the risks of business and commercial disputes. Available forms of insurance coverage include general commercial liability, commercial automobile, directors and officers, errors and omissions, and other specialized areas of coverage.

The amount of insurance protection required by a business is based upon a number of factors such as the amount of revenue generated by the company, the amount of assets owned by the company, the industry in which the company operates, the number of employees in the company, and the market value of the company. Insurance protection is a significant component of risk management in any business enterprise. An insurance professional who specializes in business coverage should be consulted to ensure adequate protection to mitigate potential liabilities as much as possible.

◼ Asset Protection

As discussed under the chapter titled "business organization," there are tremendous benefits to using multi-entity structures to leverage the risks of controlling all assets in one entity. Each segment of the business enterprise should be viewed as having its own separate existence with separate risks of liability. Therefore, using a separate business entity structure to operate separate lines of business is a good approach to risk management and business asset protection.

In reference to the personal assets of entrepreneurs, there are estate planning tools that should be considered to protect the property acquired. A detailed discussion of those tools is beyond the scope of this book, but let's briefly consider one of the options. Trusts are instruments that are now widely used for various reasons depending on the intent and desire of the persons establishing such an arrangement. Although trusts most often apply to individual formations, business trusts are recognized in some jurisdictions as a form of business entity classification.

A trust is a separately identifiable entity that is formed by an individual transferring property to one party to be held for the benefit of another. A trust is often used when a parent wishes to place certain assets in the hands of a custodial entity or person, usually referred to as a trustee, to be distributed to a third party such as their children in accordance with the terms and provisions of the trust documents. For purposes of asset identification, upon the proper formation of a viable trust, the assets are no longer owned by the transferor, but become the property of the custodial entity or trustee and thus are not generally subject to the liabilities of the transferor.

In addition to the aforementioned, there are certain states that have statutes and rules that protect the personal property of their residents from debts and liabilities. Entrepreneurs may want to consider the various legal protections available under the laws of certain jurisdictions when determining asset allocation and investment options. The same asset protection considerations should be applied to business interests. Businesses may have even greater flexibility in diversifying assets.

It is my desire that this chapter assist an entrepreneur in doing the following:

(1) obtain an awareness of the potential claims and causes of action that a business may encounter;

(2) have an awareness of the rights and options for a business in handling commercial disputes and potential claims;

(3) understand how business and commercial claims are generally resolved and the common processes relied upon to resolve them;

(4) minimize the risks of liability associated with disputes as much as possible; and

(5) obtain an awareness of ways that both business and personal assets can be better protected to minimize potential losses.

Yes, disputes may arise in your business ventures, but even those can be managed with foresight and planning.

Chapter 11

Corporate Compliance

Corporate compliance is one of the most overlooked or ignored areas related to business operation. Large and mid-size companies tend to focus their resources on areas that directly affect their revenue and profit margins. Corporate compliance functions are often placed in risk management departments. Though they are related, they are two separate categories of concern. An effective compliance program is one that has been designed to prevent and detect violations of law.

Most small business owners do not see the need to focus on compliance until it becomes a significant issue in the marketplace of their industry or a specific problem occurs within their operations. Let's face it. The core premise for entrepreneurship is to develop a business that is capable of generating revenue and manage it so that the business will be profitable. This is why compliance is most often an afterthought for ambitious entrepreneurs. However, you must not be deceived.

Any violations of the law by a business could potentially eliminate all of the profit-making potential for the business and drastically affect its revenues, especially if negative publicity is associated with the matter. Therefore, it would certainly be in the best interest of every business to manage such activities in its standard operating procedures. I believe the best way to accomplish this task is to implement a corporate compliance program that is consistent with the standard operating procedures of the business.

Even though it may not seem important in the early stages of business development, a wise businessperson should incorporate a corporate compliance plan into the business planning process that is specifically tailored to prevent violations of law within the industry in which the business will operate. In order for an organization to have an effective compliance program, the organization must show diligence in preventing and detecting violations of law. This does not mean that the compliance program must be guaranteed to do so. This simply means that the compliance program must be reasonably designed, implemented, and enforced to show diligence in creating and maintaining an effective program.

> In order for an organization to have an effective compliance program, the organization must show diligence in preventing and detecting violations of law.

There are minimum requirements for a corporate compliance program to be deemed effective. The following steps for creating a corporate compliance program could not only assist in providing a defense for your organization against potential violations of law but could also have an impact on your company's best practices for management and operations:

(1)   The organization must establish compliance standards and procedures that are to be implemented and enforced throughout the organization;

(2)   Key individuals within your organization who operate at a high level should be designated to oversee the compliance of the organization with the internal standards and procedures promulgated;

(3)   The organization must be sure to avoid delegating compliance responsibilities to persons or organizations that it knows could be involved in illegal operations;

(4)   There must be a training program in place to educate all employees about the importance of the program and familiarity with the standards and procedures related to the program;

(5)   There must also be methods to monitor and audit the program as well as company operations to ensure adherence to the standards and procedures, which includes a functional and effective internal reporting system that allows for reporting violations of the standards and procedures or any other potential violations of the law;

(6)   There must be consistent standards of enforcement of the compliance program policies. This includes the need to enforce by disciplinary action where appropriate. The key component is that the policies must be consistently enforced in order to be effective; and

(7)   The program must be designed to adequately detect and respond to any violations that may occur within the company's operations. The company must take all reasonable steps necessary to respond to any suspected violation and to prevent any such violations from occurring in the future.

We can better understand the effect of a corporate compliance program on a company's operations by discussing the relationship of the minimum components of the program to the standard operating procedures of the business. There are different laws that may specifically apply to certain industries. The program must not only deter violations of law generally but should address those compliance issues specifically associated with the operations of the company in the industry in which the company is regulated. Therefore, the structure of the program itself will actually depend on the industry in which your business operates within.

> The program must not only deter violations of law generally but should address those compliance issues specifically associated with the operations of the company in the industry in which it is regulated.

Since compliance program policies must be structured in accordance with industry-specific legal requirements, I believe it would be efficient to incorporate the terms of the policies for the corporate compliance program into the company's standard business practices. The most important ingredient in establishing compliance standards and procedures is to ensure that they are reasonably tailored to reduce the potential for violations of the law. The policies and procedures cannot be blanket generalizations. The policies must possess some form of definitive meaning directed at preventing unlawful activities and operations within a business organization.

There must also be oversight of the program at a high level within the organization. An individual within the company who directly reports to either the Chief Executive Officer or the Chief Operating Officer must perform the compliance officer responsibilities.

> There must also be oversight of the program at a high level within the organization.

The company must also make sure that those individuals delegated authority within the organization do not have a propensity to be involved in criminal activity. At a basic level, this could be accomplished by making sure that the company's human resource representatives perform criminal background checks on such employees as well as background checks that are specific to their involvement in a particular industry.

Most companies also present various training programs for their employees. Those training programs should include training on compliance topics. The overall policies and procedures for the compliance program should also be covered in training sessions not only to satisfy the training component, but also to educate the employees about the program and their obligations to operate in accordance with its policies and procedures.

Most companies require their management personnel to monitor and audit certain areas of operation to be sure that the staff is meeting the goals set forth by management. It may be possible to overlay many of the reporting features with additional lines of reporting for legal compliance issues and other matters associated with the compliance program.

However, the reporting system for corporate compliance should be uniquely structured so that employees will not be afraid to report violations of the law or compliance policies. For this reason, I recommend that the compliance program reporting system be directed to an independent representative of the company who is not within the basic general operational flow of the organizational structure. Most companies designate their corporate compliance officer to fulfill this need or give these duties to a high level executive with no direct operational oversight.

The final components for discussion, which are enforcement and prevention, are in essence the ultimate objectives of the corporate compliance program. Standards and procedures have no meaning if they are not enforced. Consequently, all directors, officers, and employees of an organization must be accountable for enforcement of the compliance standards and procedures. As discussed in the chapter on business management, managers have a responsibility to make the employees accountable for meeting certain goals and objectives in fulfilling the mission of the business. Management must also make all employees accountable for violations under the compliance program in order for it to be effective.

> Standards and procedures have no meaning if they are not enforced.

Establishing a corporate compliance program may seem to be a daunting task, but it is simply a method of documenting and managing something that should be properly managed regardless of the existence of a program, compliance with the law. Once your business has reached a level of steady growth and development, it would be wise to protect against the investment made in building the business enterprise. The value of corporate compliance could be much greater than you can imagine.

> Establishing a corporate compliance program may seem to be a daunting task, but it is simply a method of documenting and managing something that should be properly managed regardless of the existence of a program, compliance with the law.

Chapter 12

Corporate Transactions

The term "corporate transactions" is a very broad and generic phrase. For purposes of this publication, this term refers to those transactions that involve a business relationship between a business entity and one or more other business entities that affects the corporate organizational structure of the businesses that are a party to the relationship. These transactions generally occur after a business has reached a certain level of growth and development. However, it could become necessary to form such relationships in the early stages of the business.

The format and structure of corporate business arrangements that can be considered are extensive. On the other hand, there are basic corporate transaction arrangements that often form the foundation for other variations of corporate deal-making. These core transaction forms are as follows:

- Joint Ventures;
- Mergers; and
- Acquisitions

There are hybrid transactions that could be performed, but the core framework of corporate business transactions will be centered upon the transaction types delineated above.

Joint Ventures

A joint venture is best described as a single purpose operating partnership arrangement with a limited duration that is project specific. It is also important to note that a joint venture is characterized as a separate business entity for operational purposes. To this end, a joint venture exhibits many of the characteristics of a general partnership in that a joint venture operates as a separately identifiable entity, but all liability for its operations are assumed by the parties to the joint venture. As in the case of a general partnership, the joint venture structure does not afford limited liability protection to its participants as a corporation or limited liability company.

> A joint venture is best described as a single purpose operating partnership arrangement with a limited duration that is project specific.

Therefore, most joint venture arrangements consist of joint ventures between corporate entities, limited liability companies, or other entity structures that may afford the individual business representatives limited liability protection. The need to establish joint venture relationships may also be another reason for business enterprises to form separate subordinate or affiliated entities and thereby creating a multi-entity structure. The purpose of creating such structures is to isolate the potential liabilities of the joint venture arrangement from the other divisions of the business enterprise.

Joint venture arrangements are usually considered when one company believes that it may need the support of another company to complete a specific project or to obtain a potential business opportunity. Two or more companies may agree to share their efforts in a specific endeavor or on a specific project. Each company may have separate and unique areas of responsibility in handling the project.

It is common for one of the parties to the joint venture to agree to assume the responsibility of managing the project and act as the key representative for the project when dealing with third parties. There are times, however, when the parties agree to share those responsibilities. If such managerial responsibilities are shared among the joint venture parties, there must be a governing process established to address decision-making authority. All of these governance rules are set forth in the joint venture agreement.

The joint venture agreement must describe the parties to the arrangement, the name of the joint venture (if a separate name is established for the joint venture), the effective date of the joint venture, the duration of the joint venture, the project or purpose of the joint venture, the responsibilities of the parties to the joint venture, and the allocation of the ownership percentages between the joint venture parties. There are several other provisions that may be included in the joint venture agreement, but the aforementioned provisions are essential to establishing an effective joint venture.

Mergers

> **M**ergers are transactions that involve combining two or more companies into one company.

The term "merger" is often used to identify a transaction consisting of a transfer of equity and/or assets between companies at the same level of growth and development. Mergers are transactions that involve combining two or more companies to make one company. A merger is most easily characterized as two or more companies merging together to form one business entity.

There are several different reasons for companies to decide to merge. The companies may seek to:

(1) increase their pace of growth in the marketplace by consolidating assets into one viable entity,

(2) combine strengths and efforts of management capabilities within the organizations,

(3) provide greater impact in the market,

(4) produce increased leverage in dealing with competitors in the industry, and/or

(5) avail themselves to other economic benefits that could result from the consolidation of the entities.

Many of the same business reasons for mergers are also the basis for acquisitions.

Acquisitions

The term "acquisition" is more often used to identify transactions consisting of the acquisition of equity and/or assets of one company by another company. There are two methods for structuring acquisitions. One method entails the acquisition of shares of equity interest from a business by another business entity. The first matter to consider under this form of transaction is the structure of the business organizations. Is the entity to be acquired a sole proprietorship, a partnership, a limited partnership, a limited liability company, or a corporation? The structure of the acquiring entity is also significant in determining the appropriate structure of the transaction.

> The term "acquisition" is more often used to identify transactions consisting of the acquisition of equity and/or assets of one company by another company.

Obviously, an acquisition of sole proprietorships by another sole proprietorship may not be as intensive as an acquisition of corporations by another corporation. Corporations have a greater degree of formality associated with their formation and operation, and thus would require a different method of structure. The same is true for the other entity structures that have more regulatory requirements. The process for making the business deal arrangements is the same for all acquisition-related business transactions. This process is discussed in greater detail in a later section in this chapter.

The other acquisition method involves the acquisition of substantially all of the assets of one business organization by another business organization. Entity structure considerations are not as significant in this transaction structure since there is no transfer of the equity interest of the business between the parties. However, there are significant legal considerations in asset purchases. The parties first evaluate the amount and the nature of the assets to be acquired.

Many of the transaction structure considerations are based upon the types of assets being transferred. As an example, real estate transfers involve formalities and must be handled in accordance with all real estate laws and industry standards. Another highly regulated process would be the transfer of financial products and instruments. Therefore, the parties to an asset purchase transaction must evaluate the nature of the assets and properly analyze the legal principles that apply to each of the asset categories.

■ Stock Purchase Transactions

Stock purchase transactions entail the purchase of equity interest of one business by another business entity. The stock purchase could include a part or all of the issued and outstanding shares of interest in the business.

Stock purchase transactions could include various documents to reflect agreements between the parties as well as identification of interests owned or claimed by the parties. Some of the most common provisions in a stock purchase agreement are seller covenants, general representations and warranties by all parties, closing conditions that must be met prior to closing the transaction, post-closing conditions that must be met upon completion of the closing, indemnifications by the buyer and seller for liabilities associated with the business being sold, purchase price, method of financing the payment of the purchase price, and a description of the equity interest being sold. Of course, there are several other provisions included in such agreements, but I consider the aforementioned provisions to be some of the most significant.

■ Asset Purchase Transactions

This involves a company's acquisition of substantially all of the assets of another company. Of course, there are transactions that involve the sale of specific property from one company to another and do not involve the sale of substantially all of the assets of another company. But those transactions are often documented by agreements specific to the sale of the property being transferred and sold.

The focus in this chapter is on those transactions that affect the organizational structure and foundation of one or more companies. Accordingly, the transfer of substantially all of the assets of one company to another changes the operational capacity and structure of the business that is transferring its assets. It also modifies the structural dynamics of the company that is acquiring the assets.

The documents associated with asset purchase transactions could be very extensive depending upon the number assets being transferred and the nature of those assets. The asset purchase agreement is the key document for the transaction. There is also a bill of sale for the assets transferred. In addition, there are specific legal requirements for documenting the transfer of certain types of assets such real estate, financial instruments and products, bulk inventory, and other unique or regulated assets. Therefore, it is extremely important to specifically identify the assets and the legal requirements related to each asset and describe them in the pre-closing checklist prior to completing a sale of assets. This leads us to a discussion about the process for planning and completing mergers and acquisitions.

■ The Process

The process for structuring and documenting mergers and acquisitions is very similar. The initial document presented is a letter of intent. The letter of intent describes the proposal by the parties to enter into a merger or acquisition transaction. The letter of intent will generally include confidentiality provisions, or reference a separately executed confidentiality agreement, and include a formal agreement to allow the parties to begin the due diligence process.

The interested parties must first perform a due diligence review of the business structure and operations of the other interested parties to the proposed transaction. This due diligence process requires a large amount of time and effort if done appropriately and it should also be handled in an extremely thorough manner.

A complete analysis of the due diligence process is beyond the scope of this book. However, I would like to give you some basic information so that you will understand the basic framework of the process. A few of the suggested areas that should be reviewed and evaluated in the due diligence process regardless of the proposed transaction structure are delineated as follows:

- Description of the entity structure of the company and its subsidiaries and affiliates

- Organizational charts

- Background on existing directors, officers, and other key personnel

- Company policy and procedure manuals

- Company business plan

- Description of all products and services sold by the company

- Identification of all real estate owned or leased by company

- Description of all operational facilities owned or leased by company

- Most recent financial statements

- Most recent sales forecasts

After the due diligence process is completed, the parties must finalize their negotiations on the terms of the proposed transaction. Many business representatives desire to acknowledge their understanding of the proposed transaction in an amended letter of intent or term sheet. These term sheet documents will be used as the transaction map to prepare the required documentation for closing the transaction.

Upon completion of the due diligence process and the term sheet documents, it would be prudent for the parties to prepare pre-closing, closing, and post-closing checklists. Such checklists assist them in managing the flow of the transactions throughout the process. The pre-closing checklist specifies all of those items that must be completed by the parties prior to the closing of the transaction. The closing checklist describes all the documents and items that must be completed and signed at the closing to finalize the transaction.

Once the pre-closing matters have been resolved and the closing documents have been completed, the parties prepare for closing the transaction. The closing is the most anticipated event in the transaction. However, it is not the final phase of the process. There is also a post-closing phase that involves coordinating all of the transitional elements related to the transaction.

The post-closing phase also involves documenting the completion of all post-closing covenants agreed upon between the parties in the closing documents. This includes the completion of asset transfers, financing arrangements, and the basic practical requirements such as establishment of new bank accounts and other newly established components for new operations to flourish. In the end, the goal of all parties to such transactions is to facilitate an arrangement that modifies the structure and operations of business organizations in an efficient manner. If this is accomplished, the transaction has served its purpose. Once this transaction is complete, the next transaction may be on the horizon.

Chapter 13

Business Management

By this time you are probably wondering how you are going to manage all of the matters we have discussed up to this point. Well, don't despair. Remember that you are not alone. Every business must evaluate and navigate through all of the foregoing topics if it plans to exist for any significant period of time.

We are going to focus on what I believe to be the core matters of significance in the area of business management. The information that is essential to effectively managing your business is just as relevant to large corporations as it is to small businesses. I believe that the same basic framework must be structured for all business interests, and the true test of successful business management is determining how to adjust these foundational categories through all phases of the business journey, including growth and development.

Business management involves the utilization of resources in a collaborative manner in order to achieve the vision and purpose of the organization. As a foundational premise, the wise business person should establish, at a minimum, a process for managing the following:

> **B**usiness management involves the utilization of resources in a collaborative manner in order to achieve the vision and purpose of the organization.

(1) tangible assets (real and personal property),

(2) financial resources,

(3) human resources, and

(4) information or data.

Each one of these categories could effectively add value to the business organization.

Each category that is mismanaged could also lead to the degradation of the business organization and effectively reduce its value. Moreover, failure to properly manage one of the categories could have a significant effect on how the organization must manage the other basic categories of managerial concern. It could also have an enormous impact on the overall success of the business organization in fulfilling its purpose for the market.

If you are not familiar with general business management concepts and strategies, you may be wondering how to best fulfill these management responsibilities in a balanced manner without failing to address other significant matters and responsibilities as an entrepreneur. There are many theories and abstract concepts that could be presented and discussed among business professionals and academic scholars in the area of business management. However, we will focus on what I believe to be the most significant concepts and could serve as the basic foundational principles.

First, I want to point out that managing is not often a methodical one-time process. Matters must be addressed on a continuum. Managers must be able to review and modify processes and procedures on a consistent basis in order to meet the new challenges the business may face in its industry or in the marketplace.

> Managers must be able to review and modify processes and procedures on a consistent basis in order to meet the new challenges the business may face in its industry or in the marketplace.

With that in mind, let's discuss the basic management process. As you were apprised in previous chapters, business leadership must first have a vision that ignites the purpose for which the business was created. The next step is to create a plan that is designed to fulfill the purpose of the organization and the vision of its founders.

This can be accomplished by taking action in the primary managerial function, which is establishing the mission, goals, and plans for the business organization. A new entrepreneur needs to understand that the most effective way of meeting this task is to create a comprehensive business plan that can be adjusted and modified as the company develops. This area is discussed in greater detail in the chapter titled, "the plan."

During the development of a comprehensive plan for the success of the business, management should prepare an organizational chart that establishes the governing flow of internal business operations. This step is vital to the developmental growth of the enterprise.

> An organization without an organizational chart has no order or structure to function within.

Without an effective organizational chart, there can be no accountability established among the personnel, there is no framework for effective communication between departments and their personnel, and there is no foundation for a plan of action to be developed for the most appropriate and efficient use of human resources. In short, an organization without an organizational chart has no order or structure to function within.

The next key function of management is organizing all of the business resources into various categories. In the beginning phase of a business, the focus may be upon managing marketing efforts, financial resources, information, and data. As the business grows and continues to develop, the focus may turn to the management of tangible assets and human resources as areas of main concern. Regardless of the stage of business development, management must determine the need for various resources within the business and organize the resources of the business so that a continuous flow of operation will occur.

Management must also lead and motivate the people supplying their time and skill in the form of human resources to the business. Management of people is a major topic in its own right. We will not be able to cover all of the intricate matters that evolve from human relationships within the business organization.

> **M**anagement must also lead and motivate the people supplying their time and skill in the form of human resources to the business.

However, it should be acknowledged that the leadership in any organization, often personified in positions of top management in a business, has a duty to use effective methods to lead and motivate the people under the management's leadership to accomplish the goals of the organization and to work diligently to fulfill the purpose of the organization by making the vision of its founders a reality.

An additional function of management is centered on the need for establishing accountability. Management has an additional responsibility to control the structure and operations of the business in such a manner that it can evaluate progress and regulate the methods by which things are accomplished on behalf of the business organization. This has been a key component of management. Failure to effectively manage such areas

> **M**anagement has an additional esponsibility to control the structure and operations of the business.

has been linked to the failure of large corporations to comply with ethical and legal obligations, ultimately leading to their demise and subjecting their top management to possible criminal liability.

Accountability can be established through policies and procedures and/or the implementation of a corporate compliance program. Policies and procedures can manage internal functional compliance, and a corporate compliance program can manage regulatory compliance.

Regulatory compliance is reviewed in detail in the chapter titled, "corporate compliance." If management could formulate a compliance program that is designed to prevent and deter violations of the law, it could have an enormous impact on accountability standards even as a by-product. Of course, a compliance program may not directly address those accountability issues involving operational efficiency. Therefore, it is imperative for management to not only establish policies and standard operating procedures but also create methods to deter behavior that is not consistent with the vision and purpose of the organization. This may be done by establishing and publicizing the organizational chain of command and adhering to the disciplinary policies and procedures designed to regulate human resource matters.

As your business grows and develops, it will become necessary to create different levels of managerial control in order to effectively manage the day-to-day details of each area of the business. There are generally three main levels of management categories in an organization. The executive management consists of those persons who are responsible for developing the organization's purpose and vision. They also approve the policies and procedures that govern the internal processes within the organization in addition to providing effective leadership.

The general management (sometimes referred to as middle management) provides managerial support by monitoring enforcement of policies and procedures as well as the progress of their department in fulfilling the objectives of the business as directed by the executive management. General management representatives must translate the mission of the company to the operational divisions in the company. They are positioned to oversee the supervisors and report the status of project development to the executive management.

The next level of management consists of supervisors. Supervisors have direct involvement with project development and completion. They must have a thorough knowledge of the area in which they are supervising and a complete understanding of the resources required to manage the projects. They must also have good

The combination of all levels of management working cooperatively on a consistent basis and an organized flow of communication between the levels of management create an environment of organization and managed progression.

interpersonal skills in order to work closely with the staff in handling the requisite duties.

The combination of all levels of management working cooperatively on a consistent basis and an organized flow of communication between the levels of management create an environment of organization and managed progression. However, any flaw in the communications between management could result in a chaotic environment that fosters mistakes and inconsistencies. The results may not be immediate or direct in their consequences, but they will cause loss of resources, time, and money. All of which deter the fulfillment of the vision and purpose of any business organization.

Management can be the greatest asset in a business. It could also be the greatest liability if not performed properly. An investment in establishing an efficient management system could not only limit losses but could increase the value of the business organization.

ACTION

①②③④**5**

Chapter 14

Success:
The Journey Never Ends

This ideology could be summed up in one word: Action! In the journey analogy, this factor simply means to take the journey that you have prepared for so exhaustively. It is the next logical step after you have designed your purpose, vision, map, and plan for your business. No matter what you have accomplished up to this level of preparation, you must be willing to take the necessary action to reach the points of destination you have purposely envisioned.

Most people are familiar with the cliché, "Lights, Camera, Action." Well, if you really think about it, there is a lot of preparation that goes into an entertainment show before it is presented to the public. But the most important aspect of show business is the ability to perform and produce, in other words, the ability to take action. The same is true for any business. No product or service can be produced unless action is taken. Consumers

> No matter what you have accomplished up to this level of preparation, you must be willing to take the necessary action to reach the points of destination you have purposely envisioned.

cannot enjoy the benefits of the company's products or services until

> **U**ltimately the vision and purpose have no meaning unless action is taken.

action is taken. Ultimately, the vision and purpose have no meaning unless action is taken.

As with all meaningful journeys in life, this is a journey that you will never forget. I believe the journeys in entrepreneurship are similar to those in life. We must be willing to pursue our passions in spite of our fears and the obstacles that stand before us.

However, to grow and develop a business enterprise, the person needs to understand several other concepts that can guide and implement its operations. In other words, you would serve yourself well to make every effort to understand the business of doing business.

After recognizing and understanding the business of doing business, you can better position your company for growth, development, and rewarding economic success. If the company does not reach its expected destination of success in business, don't panic. Simply remind yourself of your entrepreneurship map, and you can always start on a new journey with its own newfound purpose. Your destination for each new journey in business remains the same. The destiny

> **W**e must be willing to pursue our passions in spite of our fears and the obstacles that stand before us.

for your business interests should always be to successfully manifest the vision and purpose for which the business is formed.

The entrepreneurial spirit can be an extension of your passion to create for the people of the world something that has a significant meaning to them and to you. It could be your desire to pursue your passions with unlimited potential. On the other hand, it could be simply your determination to accomplish a task that you believe you were purposely placed on this earth to accomplish.

However you define your entrepreneurial heart, remember that it can continue to beat through business failures, financial losses, and unforeseen circumstances. The end of one business venture could lead to the beginning of another. The demise of one of your companies could actually be designed to steer your passions in another direction to fulfill a new vision and purpose for new expectations along the journey.

> However you define your entrepreneurial heart, remember that it can continue to beat through business failures, financial losses, and unforeseen circumstances.

Entrepreneurship is not defined by your specific business ideas for the existing business climate. Entrepreneurship is your ability to discover passion, define a purpose, create a vision, develop a plan, follow the map, and take action to pursue opportunities of unlimited potential. Entrepreneurship is a continuum of ideas and

> **S**uccess in entrepreneurship is based upon your continuous movement through the unending journey of undeterred passionate pursuit of business endeavors to serve society.

actions motioning toward a common objective. Accordingly, in my opinion, success in entrepreneurship is accomplished by simply being an entrepreneur, regardless of the ultimate outcomes.

Always strive to be the best. Always work diligently to achieve the best. After all, if any purpose is true to your passions, it is definitely worth fulfilling. Always plan to take your vision completely through and to its points of destination, knowing that you have a knowledge map and a strategic plan. You must know that it can and will be done. We are ready to take a journey to a world of opportunities. Opportunities will lead to opportunities. This means we should continue to face this journey

Never be discouraged in your endless pursuit of success in entrepreneurship in spite of the obstacles and failures along the way. Success in entrepreneurship is not based upon the final destination of any particular business endeavor. Success in entrepreneurship is based upon your continuous movement through the unending journey of undeterred passionate pursuit of business endeavors to serve society. If you have a heart for entrepreneurship, live in your passion to do business and enjoy the journey. The true entrepreneurial destination is the place where you embrace the reality that the joy is in the journey, and the journey never ends.

About the Author

DARWIN J. BRUCE, J.D.

Mr. Darwin J. Bruce is an entrepreneurship and business strategist. Mr. Bruce has been honored by the Dallas Business Journal as a "Forty under 40" honoree, which recognizes the top 40 business executives and entrepreneurs under the age of forty in the Dallas/Fort Worth area. In 2009, he was a recipient of a *Distinguished Alumni Award* from SMU Dedman School of Law. Mr. Bruce was also recently featured in D CEO Magazine. Mr. Bruce works with entrepreneurs, business executives, and business leaders in their quest to manage all of the matters affecting corporate structure, strategic planning, and operations of their organizations. He has been a guest speaker at Business Management Seminars across the country. Topics presented in prior speaking engagements included leadership, professional growth and development, entrepreneurship, strategic business development and planning, mergers and acquisitions, and corporate compliance. He has also been a lecturer in the areas of business law and business management. He is a certified Entrepreneur Trainer and Instructor and the author of a book titled, "*The Map to Entrepreneurship.*"

Mr. Bruce is the Chief Operating Officer for The Potter's House of Dallas, Inc., a globally recognized multicultural, nondenominational organization of more than 30,000 members located in Dallas, Texas founded by Bishop T.D. Jakes. He is responsible for managing all of the business affairs for the organization and its affiliated entities. In addition, he serves as Chairman of the Metroplex Economic Development Corporation, an affiliated non-profit organization that provides individuals, families, and entrepreneurs with tools and strategies to with tools and strategies to help them achieve economic empowerment through various programs. He is also an adjunct professor on Business Strategy and Entrepreneurship at Southern Methodist University in Dallas, Texas.

Mr. Bruce has experience in all phases of business organization and management. He has served as Chief Executive Officer for an electronic manufacturing and service company. He has also served as Vice President and General Counsel for health care and finance companies in previous years.

Mr. Bruce received his Juris Doctor degree from SMU School of Law and holds a Bachelor's degree from Texas A&M University. He serves on the Executive Board of Directors of SMU School of Law and on the Advisory Board of Directors of SMU School of Engineering.

Darwin J. Bruce
P.O. Box 540162
Dallas, Texas 75354
www.darwinbruce.com

CPSIA information can be obtained at www.ICGtesting.com
Printed in the USA
BVOW080443100413

317761BV00002B/5/P